RON KLINGER ANSWERS YOUR BRIDGE QUERIES

Ron Klinger

CASSELL
IN ASSOCIATION WITH
PETER CRAWLEY

First published in Great Britain 2004
in association with Peter Crawley
by Cassell
Wellington House, 125 Strand, London WC2R 0BB
an imprint of the Orion Publishing Group

A catalogue record for this book
is available from the British Library

ISBN 0304 36673 0

Typeset by Modern Bridge Publications
P.O. Box 140, Northbridge NSW 1560, Australia

Printed in Great Britain by
Clays Ltd, St Ives plc

CONTENTS

Introduction

From time to time players contact me with situations that caused them difficulty at the bridge table. In the old days the queries were by ordinary mail and they were sporadic. With the advent of email the inquiries have become more frequent. It is of constant interest to peruse these and see the misconceptions, misunderstandings and problems plaguing regular club players.

The writers often apologise for writing, saying they hope I do not mind them bothering me. Often they end with something like, 'If you are too busy to answer this, we'll understand'. Busy though I might be, I have always answered and do not mind doing so. Part of the aim of bridge teachers and bridge writers is to improve the standard of their audience. If the players writing to us are keen enough to ask and to seek advice, how could we not try to help and point them in the right direction?

Bidding seems to give players far more headaches than the play of the cards. Questions on bidding would outnumber play problems twenty to one. The material was voluminous and this has been reduced to those queries and answers which seem to be the most useful, most common and most interesting. They have been divided by subject matter, including opening bids, responses, competitive bidding, slam bidding, those dealing with conventions and leads, play and defence.

Virtually every letter has been edited to remove irrelevant details and social niceties and thus pruned to the bare essentials. In some instances the replies have also been edited, sometimes to reduce the content, other times to clarify or explain the position in greater detail.

The letters themselves appear in italics, the answers in ordinary (Roman) type. Some have only one query and are thus easy to answer. Others contain a number of questions and some of them are contingent on the reply to the initial query. For these it is easier to give the answers as we go along. In that case you will see '*(continuing)*', which starts a new section of the letter. After the answer, players sometimes write back with further details and these are included starting with '*Reply*' or '*Follow-up*'.

The answers are essentially the same as the actual original reply. Occasionally there have been second thoughts or other ideas and these are included under '*Post script*'. In the chapter on conventions, the usage and meaning of the convention are explained before the answer.

Some of the chapters start with or include later questions on which to test yourself. To obtain the maximum benefit from the material you should decide on your own answers to these questions before referring to the letters themselves.

Those writers whom I could contact were asked whether they would like to have their name included or whether they wished to remain anonymous. That is why you will sometimes see full names, sometimes initials only and sometimes '*Name withheld*'.

The material here covers a wide range of bridge problems. You can delve anywhere and are bound to find something that will be of interest and which could improve your own game.

Happy bridging.

Ron Klinger,
2004

Chapter 1: Should I open with this junk?

What action would you take with these hands?

1. Dealer, game all *(see page 10)*
    - ♠ K Q
    - ♡ J 9 8 3
    - ◇ K Q 10 9 6 5
    - ♣ 5

2. Dealer, teams, love all *(see page 10)*
    - ♠ 2
    - ♡ Q 10 9 8 7 6 5 2
    - ◇ 8 5
    - ♣ Q 6

3. Teams, vulnerable, pass on your right *(see page 11)*
    - ♠ J 9 2
    - ♡ A 10 9 4
    - ◇ A J 9 7 2
    - ♣ Q

4. Dealer, teams, not vulnerable vs. vulnerable *(see page 12)*
    - ♠ J 9 6 3
    - ♡ 10
    - ◇ K Q J 7 6 2
    - ♣ K 2

A good guide for opening with a one-bid (and more accurate than the Rule of 20) is: Add HCP + the number of cards in your two longest suits + your quick tricks. If the total is 22+ always open. With 21+, open at favourable vulnerability.

The 22+ requirement is mildly conservative and 21½ or more (and 20½ or more at favourable vulnerability) is a reasonable standard. The quick trick scale counts the tricks you will probably make on the first two rounds of a suit. These are tricks that you are likely to win whether as declarer or in defence.

A-K = 2, A-Q = 1½, A = 1, K-Q = 1, K = ½ if not singleton.

Hi, Ron,
My friend . . . had:

♠ K Q
♥ J 9 8 3
♦ K Q 10 9 6 5
♣ 5

He passed, don't know why, but he says, 'after reading your book, When To Bid, When To Pass'. Do you agree with him?

Eva of London, England

Answer: Definitely worth a 1♦ opening.

Postscript: Counting 11 HCP + 10 cards in two suits + 2 quick tricks = 23. Deduct 1 for the K-Q doubleton still leaves 22, enough to justify a one-opening. A further problem featuring this hand can be found on page 62.

Hi, Ron,
Playing teams, nil vulnerable, I held as dealer:

♠ 2
♥ Q 10 9 8 7 6 5 2
♦ 8 5
♣ Q 6

I opened 4♥, pass, pass, 4♠ from RHO which partner doubled for +500. I feel 4♥ is pushy, but surely it is worth 3♥, or at least 2♦, showing a weak 6-card major. Pass sounds too wimpish for words.

George Biro of Sydney, Australia

Answer: These days 4♡ is routine. Maybe 10-15 years ago one would open 3♡. The 4♡ opening is supposed to be weak and the 8-card suit tilts it to 4♡ rather than 3♡. Similarly you should open 4♠ at love all or favourable vulnerability with:

♠ Q 10 9 6 4 3 2
♡ - - -
◇ 8 5
♣ K 9 8 2

Dear Ron,
My partner and I being devotees of your When to Bid, When to Pass advice, which we endeavour to abide by at all times, the following hand raised some heated discussion:
Teams, vulnerable, pass on your right

♠ J 9 2
♡ A 10 9 4
◇ A J 9 7 2
♣ Q

Is this an opening hand? What value, if any do you give to the singleton ♣Q?

(Name withheld)

Answer: Yes, it is an opening hand. Bid 1◇. You have 12 HCP + 9 cards in 2 suits + 2 Quick tricks = 23. Deducting 1 point for the singleton honour still leaves 22 and that is enough for a respectable opening. For a singleton K, Q or J, deduct 1 point from the total value of the hand.
Postscript: A singleton honour can be useful or useless depending on what partner holds in the suit. Facing 10-x-x or worse, a singleton queen has no value, but facing holdings such as K-J-x, A-J-x, A-K-J-x, the singleton queen is worth much more than a singleton low card.

Hi, Ron,

1st seat, not vulnerable against vulnerable, you hold as East:

♠ J 9 6 3
♡ 10
♢ K Q J 7 6 2
♣ K 2

Do you open? You have a weak 2 ♢ available if you like.

I. McK., Australia

Answer: I open 1 ♢. In raw form, HCP + two longest suits + quick tricks = 21½ = opening one-bid. Adjusting for jack with two higher honours = +½, so total opening points = 22.

I.McK.: If you open 1 ♢, it goes 2 ♡ (weak) on your left, pass, pass to you. Do you re-open with a double?

Answer: Yes. If short in their suit, do not pass.

I.McK.: I passed 2 ♡ out. We picked up with our 300 against their 180! This was the full deal:

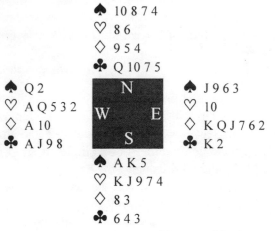

```
              ♠ 10 8 7 4
              ♡ 8 6
              ♢ 9 5 4
              ♣ Q 10 7 5
♠ Q 2              N              ♠ J 9 6 3
♡ A Q 5 3 2   W       E          ♡ 10
♢ A 10                           ♢ K Q J 7 6 2
♣ A J 9 8         S              ♣ K 2
              ♠ A K 5
              ♡ K J 9 7 4
              ♢ 8 3
              ♣ 6 4 3
```

Postscript: South should bid 1♡, not 2♡, and East needs to double to compensate East-West for the game available.

Chapter 2: What opening bid should I choose?

What action would you take with these hands?

1. Dealer, playing 1NT as 12-14 *(see pages 15-17)*
   ♠ A 7
   ♡ Q 8 6 4 2
   ♢ A K 3
   ♣ 8 6 2

2. Dealer, playing standard Acol *(see page 17)*
   ♠ J
   ♡ Q J 9 7 6 3 2
   ♢ - - -
   ♣ A J 10 9 8

3. Dealer, game all *(see pages 17-18)*
   ♠ K Q J 9 8 6 4 3 2
   ♡ - - -
   ♢ K Q 8 7
   ♣ - - -

4. Second-in-hand, game all. RHO opens 1♣ *(see page 19)*
   ♠ A K 5 3
   ♡ K Q J 10 9 8 7 5 4 2
   ♢ - - -
   ♣ - - -

Dear Ron,

Quite a number of people here play that opening 1♠ promises at least five cards, 1♡ at least four. I can understand the reasons why many prefer 5-card majors, but cannot see the logic in opening 1♠ with 5+, but not 1♡.

Alice McIntosh of Capetown, South Africa

Answer: Most of the bridge world, including me, prefer 5-card majors rather than 5+ for spades and 4+ for hearts. Still, the 1♠ = five, 1♡ = four approach is not foolish and does have some benefits. Those who play it do so because it is more 'natural' to open 1♡ when holding 4-4 in the majors rather than 1♣ or 1♢ on a 3-card suit.

Most who play this way open 1♡ on a 4-card suit only if holding four spades as well. It follows that 1♣ will be a 3-card suit only when holding four spades or four hearts in a 4-3-3-3 pattern and the 1♢ opening will always be a 4+ suit.

It also follows that if a 1♡ opener denies four spades, then 5+ hearts are promised. For example, if the bidding commences 1♡ : 1♠, 1NT or 1♡ : 1♠, 2♣ / 2♢, opener is showing at least five hearts.

A significant downside comes when the opponents overcall after the 1♡ opening. If it starts 1♡ : (3♢), it can be tricky for responder to decide whether to support hearts with three trumps or not.

Ron,

An argument has arisen about the principle of bidding 4-card suits 'up-the-line' where, using a 12-14 1NT, opener has a balanced hand above 14 HCP and the 4-card suits are a minor and a major, i.e., where you plan to re-bid NT at the suitable level later.

14

In this case do you open the minor before the major (bidding up-the-line) and on the next round bid no-trumps, thus ignoring the major?

(Name withheld)

Answer: It is usually not critical whether you open the 4-card major or the 4-card minor with a 4-4-3-2 pattern in the 15-19 range. With 4-4 in the majors it is important to open 1♡. With 4-4 in the minors you can open the stronger minor to show partner where your strength lies, but occasionally open the weaker minor to try to mislead the opponents so that they will not lead that suit.

With major-minor as your 4-card suits, it is not wise to open a weak 4-card major with 15-16 points if partner is apt to raise to 2-major with three trumps. With greater strength you can rebid 2NT or 3NT.

With a clear-cut stopper in every suit, by all means open the major, since you can rebid no-trumps if there is interference. If there is one suit unguarded (which an opponent might overcall), you need to be confident that you will have a sensible call available on the next round. As long as you play double for takeout at the one- or two-level, then you are unlikely to be in trouble whichever suit you open. It is important to remember that if you open in a major and rebid in a minor, partner will expect 5+ cards in the major.

Dear Mr. Klinger,
  Playing a weak 1NT, holding a minimum hand (12-15 points) with 5 hearts, 2 spades, 3 diamonds and 3 clubs I am struggling with what I should re-bid if I open 1♡ and responder replies 1♠? Repeating a major after a one-level response indicates a 6+ heart suit, so this is not available.

15

Bidding 2♠ is not attractive with only 2 spades. Also, re-bidding 1NT is not an option when a weak 1NT is played (because it indicates 15+ points). Is it the case that opener should not open hearts, but should rather open 1NT with the hope that responder seeks a major fit through Stayman? Or should opener's rebid of 2♡ over a 1♠ response show only five hearts, as it would over a 2♣ / 2◊ response? The former option would seem to be more attractive where the heart suit is poor quality, but not where most points (say A-K, A-K-Q or A-K-J) are held in hearts. With most points in hearts, 1NT would be dangerous and a 2♡ re-bid the only option.

Trevor Bull of St Albans, England

Answer: You have three basic options, which you need to sort out before you open:

(a) Open 1NT despite the 5-card major

(b) Open 1♡ and rebid 2♡ if the hearts are very strong

(c) Open 1♡ and rebid in a 3-card minor

Of these (a) is the most attractive since the hand is balanced. Even if the hearts are very strong, this is not a drawback. You would open 1NT if holding:

♠ 6 3 2
♡ 8 7
◊ K 8 6
♣ A K Q 6 4

so why not if the 5-card suit is hearts. *Bid Better, Much Better After Opening 1NT* has a full chapter on the advantages of opening 1NT rather than 1♡ or 1♠ when holding a 5-3-3-2 with a 5-card major and the appropriate strength.

If you do not like (a), then (b) is reasonable if the suit contains four honours. K-Q-J-10-x, A-K-J-10-x or similar is as good as a 6-card suit.

16

If the suit is weak, then you could try (c), bidding your stronger 3-card minor. For example:

♠ A 7
♡ Q 8 6 4 2
♢ A K 3
♣ 8 6 2

You could open 1♡ and rebid 2♢ over 1♠, but my advice would be to open 1NT.

Dear Ron,

Playing standard Acol, would you say that this hand had eight playing tricks and could be opened with a bid of 2♡?

♠ J
♡ Q J 9 7 6 3 2
♢ - - -
♣ A J 10 9 8

(Name withheld)

Answer: No, an Acol 2♡ opening should have not just 8-9 playing tricks, but also about 16 HCP or more. If lower, open 1♡ or make a pre-emptive bid. As it is recommended that a 1-opening should have about two quick tricks, the given hand is more suitable for a 4♡ opening.

From Elena Jeronimidis, editor of Bridge Plus magazine:

A Bridge Plus reader, David Hughes, has asked for a verdict from our pundits. You are dealer at Game All, holding:

♠ K Q J 9 8 6 4 3 2
♡ - - -
♢ K Q 8 7
♣ - - -

What do you bid? Please also say why.

Answer: Such hands are largely guesswork. Playing natural methods, I would choose 1♠ (and hope to buy the hand in spades doubled at some level), but 5♠ (bid six, partner, with any top honour in spades) is an acceptable choice. The hand is too strong for 4♠ (might miss slam), but I could accept 4♠ as long as you bid 5♠ over any action they take.

Playing the Kabel 3NT opening, one of my favourite methods, (see *Bridge Conventions, Defences and Countermeasures*), you would open 3NT (specific ace ask). That would tell you whether you belong in game, slam or grand slam. Not only is 3NT effective for the problem posed, but it is also almost as pre-emptive as 4♠.

In *Bridge Plus*, the majority voted for a 1♠ opening, with David Bird opting for 5♠, as above, and Andrew Kambites choosing 4NT as the specific ace-ask. This was the full deal:

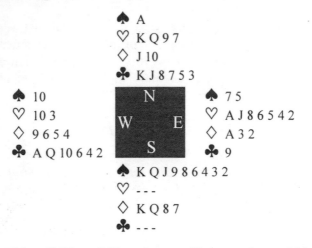

```
                    ♠ A
                    ♡ K Q 9 7
                    ◇ J 10
                    ♣ K J 8 7 5 3
     ♠ 10                            ♠ 7 5
     ♡ 10 3           N              ♡ A J 8 6 5 4 2
     ◇ 9 6 5 4    W       E          ◇ A 3 2
     ♣ A Q 10 6 4 2       S          ♣ 9
                    ♠ K Q J 9 8 6 4 3 2
                    ♡ ---
                    ◇ K Q 8 7
                    ♣ ---
```

Either 3NT or 4NT as the specific ace-ask would locate the ♠A with North and reach the lucky but laydown 6♠.

The next question is not about an opening bid, but because the hand is so similar to the previous one, it is appropriate to include it here.

Dear Ron,
What do you consider is the best sequence to reach 7 ♡ after East opens 1 ♣?

Dealer East : Game all

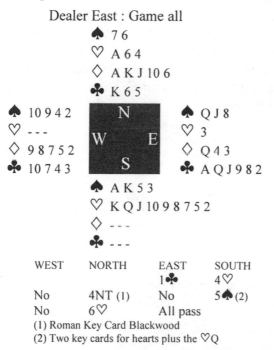

```
                    ♠ 7 6
                    ♡ A 6 4
                    ◇ A K J 10 6
                    ♣ K 6 5
  ♠ 10 9 4 2            N            ♠ Q J 8
  ♡ - - -         W         E        ♡ 3
  ◇ 9 8 7 5 2                        ◇ Q 4 3
  ♣ 10 7 4 3            S            ♣ A Q J 9 8 2
                    ♠ A K 5 3
                    ♡ K Q J 10 9 8 7 5 2
                    ◇ - - -
                    ♣ - - -
```

WEST	NORTH	EAST	SOUTH
		1♣	4♡
No	4NT (1)	No	5♠ (2)
No	6♡	All pass	

(1) Roman Key Card Blackwood
(2) Two key cards for hearts plus the ♡Q

My partner was worried that I had the ♣A and not the ♡A. No one bid the grand but 6NT was not as good as 6 ♡ + one.

Bill Turner of Bridgend, Wales

Answer: Such freak hands are usually just guesswork, but some pertinent comments can still be made.

9-4 hands are not within the framework of any textbook and so I cannot give you any sensible, natural sequence to reach 7♡ after East's opening bid. Still, the jump to 4♡ does not do the hand justice when you have a two-loser hand. Without prior discussion one might bid 6♡ at once (quite a gamble, because of the spades) or 5♡ (as long as that invites 6♡ and is not taken as just a pre-empt).

Without the 1♣ opening, South might start with 3NT as a specific ace ask (see page 18) and that should lead to 7♡. After the 1♣ opening it would be interesting to have agreements as to the meaning of 4NT (simply aces or specific aces?) and to 4♣ as well. Would (1♣) : 4♣ be a natural pre-empt after they have opened the suit showing four cards there? Could it be exclusion Blackwood with a club void? The latter method might find 7♡ this way:

WEST	NORTH	EAST	SOUTH
		1♣	4♣ (1)
No	4NT (2)	No	5♣ (3)
No	5♡ (4)	No	7♡
No	No	No	

(1) Asking for key cards outside clubs
(2) Two key cards outside clubs (must be ♡A + ◇A)
(3) Asking for kings outside clubs
(4) One king outside clubs

You will need a firm agreement about the meaning of a jump to the four-level in the opposition's suit. Since such a bid occurs so rarely, there is plenty of scope for disaster. Without prior discussion, the jump to 4♣ and the 5♣ rebid sound very 'natural' and I would hate partner to pass 5♣! After 4♣ : 4NT, perhaps South would be better off using 5NT for kings outside clubs.

Chapter 3: What is my best response?

What action would you take in these situations?

1. Pairs, Dealer North : Love all	What should South do with:
West North East South 1♡ No ? *(See pages 22-23)*	♠ J 6 4 2 ♡ 6 ◇ A 10 8 6 ♣ 8 6 4 2

2. Teams, Dealer North : E-W vul.	South's action with:
West North East South 1◇ 2♣ ? *(See pages 23-24)*	♠ Q 9 4 ♡ K 7 3 2 ◇ Q 10 6 5 ♣ J 7

3. Teams, Dealer South : Love all	What should South do with:
West North East South No No 1◇ 1♠ ? *(See page 25)*	♠ - - - ♡ J 8 6 4 3 2 ◇ 9 5 ♣ A K 7 5 4

4. Teams, Dealer North : N-S vul.	South's bidding plan with:
West North East South 1NT (1) No ? (1) 15-17 *(See page 26)*	♠ 8 7 5 4 2 ♡ J ◇ K ♣ A Q 9 6 5 4

5. Teams, Dealer North : N-S vul.	South's bidding plan with:
West North East South 1NT (1) No ? (1) 15-18 *(See page 27)*	♠ - - - ♡ 8 7 2 ◇ A K 8 6 5 ♣ Q J 7 4 3

Hello, Ron,

Playing with a new partner I proposed Drury (nobody plays it at club level in Germany) and he asked why one couldn't just bid normally, especially with a fit in partner's major, such as No : (No) : 1 ♡ : (No), 2 ♡ or 3 ♡?

BM of Heidelberg, Germany

Answer: Drury aims to keep the bidding one level lower. This can be useful if partner has made a light or super-light opening in third seat. Rather than No : 1♡, 3♡ the Drury sequence would be:

No : 1♡
2♣ : 2◇
2♡ : No

There are a number of variations for 2♣ Drury (an artificial 2♣ response by a passed hand). I like the version where 2♣ shows a maximum pass and does not guarantee support for opener. Then a 2◇ rebid by opener is artificial and shows any minimum opening, while other rebids by opener are natural and forcing to game.

Hello, Ron,

In a major tournament with 75 pairs, including several of the German bridge elite, my partner opened 1 ♡. I held:
♠ J 6 4 2
♡ 6
◇ A 10 8 6
♣ 8 6 4 2

I passed and so did my left-hand opponent. We went one or two off. Almost every one else made 4 ♠. Would you have bid 1 ♠? My partner obviously believes I should have, but I see no reason to change basic principles.

BM of Heidelberg, Germany

Answer: Yes, a 1♠ response is sensible. There are several examples in *When To Bid, When To Pass* (pages 39-40) where the advice is, 'It usually pays to respond with 4-5 HCP if you are short in opener's suit.' No one can guarantee you eternal happiness if you respond with the South cards, but nothing ventured, nothing gained. As long as the partnership can accept losses, you should respond with such a hand.

BM later advised that the full deal was:

```
                    ♠ A K Q 7
                    ♡ A 10 7 4
                    ◇ K 5
                    ♣ Q 10 7
        ♠ 3                          ♠ 10 9 8 5
        ♡ K Q 9 5 2     N            ♡ J 8 3
        ◇ J 7 2     W       E        ◇ Q 9 4 3
        ♣ K J 9 5       S            ♣ A 3
                    ♠ J 6 4 2
                    ♡ 6
                    ◇ A 10 8 6
                    ♣ 8 6 4 2
```

Even on a trump lead, declarer has a comfortable path to ten tricks in 4♠ by ruffing the heart losers in the South hand.

Hi, Ron,

You hold: *After 1 ◇ : (2 ♣) to you, do we pass and*
♠ Q 9 4   *hope for a re-opening double by partner and*
♡ K 7 3 2   *then bid 2 ♡, allowing partner to draw the*
◇ Q 10 6 5   *inference that our first-round inaction was*
♣ J 7   *based on a lack of 4-4 in the majors, or do*
we double in the first place and correct 2 ♠ to 3 ◇?

                  Neil Hayward of Capetown, South Africa

Answer: To pass first and bid 2♡ after a re-opening double (if there is one) would suggest a weaker hand than this. To double is risky, not so much if partner bids 2♠, but if the bidding escalates and partner then bids spades at a higher level. Your best move is to respond 2◇. With a strong hand partner can bid on and you would raise a 2♡ rebid to 3♡.

Hi, Ron,
(a) In one of your books you reported a deal played at a high level of competition where the sequence 1♣ : (1 ♡) : Double specifically denied four spades. Is this normal?

(b) Does 1♣ : (1 ◇) : Double promise both majors? If yes, do we have to bid 4- or 5-card major suits ambiguously if not holding 4-4? What about 1 ◇ : (2♣) : Double?
Neil Hayward of Capetown, South Africa

Answer: (a) Whether one plays 1♣/1◇ : (1♡) Double as showing four spades or denying four spades is a matter of partnership agreement. The advantage of using Double to show four spades is that a 1♠ response then shows 5+ spades. The thinking behind Double denying four spades goes like this: We can manage without any discomfort the 1♠ response to 1♣ or 1◇ as showing 4+ spades. Hence we can equally manage 1♣/1◇ : (1♡) : 1♠ as 4+ spades. Double can then be used over 1♡ to show the awkward hand types without four spades, in particular the hand which has the strength for a 1NT response but no stopper in hearts as well as the hand with length in the other minor, but too weak for a two-level response.
(b) 1♣ : (1◇) : Double should promise 4-4 majors. Likewise for 1◇ : (2♣) : Double. With only one major, just bid it over 1◇. This is no more ambiguous than 1♣ : 1♡ or 1♣ : 1♠.

Hi, Ron,
(a) At Imps, nil vulnerable, you hold:

♠ - - -
♡ J 8 6 4 3 2
◇ 9 5
♣ A K 7 5 4

Playing Acol Twos I passed as dealer and it is your call after
No : (No) : 1 ◇ : (1 ♠). I chose Double (negative).

Answer: Why not bid 2♡? The shape makes up for the slight lack of high card strength and you do have two quick tricks. You are on lead against a spade contract and need not be concerned about partner leading your rotten suit, unless LHO ventures into no-trumps.

The danger with doubling is that you may not be able to show both your heart length and the club suit later in the auction. If you bid 2♡ and it goes (2♠) : No : (No) back to you, a 3♣ rebid will have done close to justice for this hand.

(b) The bidding continued:

West	North	East	South
			No
No	1◇	1♠	Dble
2♠	3♣	No	?

Should I force to game? If yes, then should I make a courtesy splinter bid of 4 ♠?

Nick Fahrer of Sydney, Australia

Answer: You should definitely force to game and the splinter is not just a courtesy bid. You should have real ambitions for this hand. After partner bid 3♣, slam is more likely than not.

Partner had: ♠ K Q 5   ♡ A   ◇ A K 7 4 3   Q J 6 3
and slam made easily.

Dear Ron Klinger,

(a) In Chapter 19 of 'Guide to Better Acol Bridge' you advocate showing 6-card suits before 5-card suits. Fine, but what about in response?

Answer: (a) Normally the same, as long as you are strong enough to bid both suits naturally.

(b) My partner opened 1NT (15-17), vulnerable, and I held:

♠ 8 7 5 4 2

♡ J

♢ K

♣ A Q 9 6 5 4

The bidding went 1NT : 2♠ (transfer to clubs), 3♣ : 4♣ (key card for clubs), 4♠ : 5♣ (two key cards missing). We made 5♣, but almost everyone was in 4♠ plus one. My partner upbraided me for even considering clubs despite holding six cards and said I should have transferred to the five-card spade suit. With six losers opposite 15-17 I was looking for a slam and needed less support in clubs than in spades. Have you any advice for us?

Answer (b): Yes. Firstly, do not upbraid each other no matter how strong the provocation. Secondly, with a two-suiter, it is usually best to show both your suits. Your sequence might go 1NT : 2♠ (transfer to clubs), 3♣ : 3♠ (natural), 3NT : 4♠ (natural, thus showing five spades and hence longer clubs). That is as much as your hand is worth. Partner will recognise that red suit aces are golden and holdings such as ♡K-J or ♢Q-J are useless. In addition partner needs excellent cards in spades for slam to be likely. ♠A-x-x would not do.

Having bothered to introduce clubs indicates slam interest. If partner supports clubs or spades after 3♠, you are entitled to be enthusiastic about slam.

Dear Ron,

Playing duplicate, my partner opened 1NT (15-18), next player passed and I had:

♠ - - -
♡ 8 7 2
◇ A K 8 6 5
♣ Q J 7 4 3

We do not play transfers. We play 2 ◇ as (0-8 points), 3 ◇ as 13+ HCP, forcing to game with slam interest and 5 ◇ as 9-12 HCP with 6+ cards, no slam interest. I replied 2 ◇. Partner passed (she had ◇Q-x-x-x) and we made five. I was reluctant to bid 2NT with the void in spades (partner had ♠Q-x-x). Could you kindly tell me what I should have done?

Caroline Vear of Melbourne, Australia

Answer: The hand is a real problem with the methods you play. There are ways to show the hand you have, but it does require methods that are not simple and natural.

Having said that, you are better off to bid more than less. Take a chance at the big reward. You chose 2◇, a weakness bid, when you had 10 HCP and two five-card suits, enough for game. Incidentally, I would play 2◇ as 0-7, not 0-8. With most 8 HCP hands, you are worth an invitation to game.

You might have bid 3NT (which is likely to fail, but is still better than just 2◇). How about 1NT : 3◇? That need show no more than 10 HCP if the hand is very shapely, such as yours. If partner supports to 4◇, bid 5◇, denying interest in slam, or cue-bid 4♠ to suggest slam prospects.

If the bidding goes 1NT : 3◇, 3NT you can then jump to 5♣ (no slam interest) or bid 4♣ to show clubs and slam potential. If partner has a doubleton in diamonds, she will have three, four or five clubs.

Chapter 4: Problems later in the auction

Dear Ron,
  If partner opens 1 ♢ and my response is 1 ♠, is a 2 ♣ rebid by partner forcing?   *Name withheld*

Answer: 1 ♢ : 1 ♠, 2 ♣ is not forcing in standard methods. To show clubs and force responder to bid again, opener would need to jump to 3 ♣. Some play 1 ♢ : 1 ♠, 3 ♣ as artificial, a splinter raise of spades, and in that case opener's 2 ♣ rebid would be forcing. Even if 2 ♣ is not forcing, responder should pass only with 3+ clubs and 5-7 points. With 8+ points, responder should rebid, even giving false preference to 2 ♢ with a doubleton.

Hi,
  I am canvassing opinions dealing with reverses. The auction goes 1 ♡ : 2 ♣, 2 ♠. Do you agree that because responder bid 2 ♣, the 2 ♠ reverse can show fewer points than what we normally expect from a reverse?
                    Ellen Pomer, known online as 'Caitlin'

Answer: No. 2 ♠ should still show the normal values for a reverse, forcing to game after a two-over-one response. Normal here is 16+ points, perhaps shaded to a good 15 after a two-over-one, since you want to be in game with 15 opposite 10+.

  If I open 1 ♠ and partner responds, can I call 2 ♡ with only four cards in that suit? My friends say that after a 1 ♠ call, you cannot make a second call with only four cards in hearts. You must have five cards.   *(Name withheld)*

Answer: Opener's 2♥ in 1♠ : 2♣, 2♥ or 1♠ : 2◇, 2♥ is not the same as a 2♥ response to a 1♠ opening. Opener does not promise five hearts for the 2♥ *rebid*. A 4-card suit of any quality is quite acceptable. Opener will normally bid the hearts a second time to show 5-5 in spades and hearts.

The sequence 1♠ : 2♥ does show 5+ hearts with responder. The advantage of that approach is that if responder repeats the suit it will promise a 6-card suit and opener can support with a doubleton. Thus you can reach a 5-3 or 6-2 heart fit easily. With only four hearts and enough to respond at the two-level, responder would bid 2♣ or 2◇ and give opener a chance to show a 4-card heart suit.

Dear Ron,

My partner opened 1 ◇, next player passed. I bid 1 ♠ (I had nine points, five spades, no other suit). The next player passed and my partner bid 2 ♣, the next player again passed and I bid 2 ♠ (nothing else to say). My partner passed and I played it in 2 ♠ and went one down. Afterwards she told me that as responder when I repeated my spades I had to have six of them. I've never heard that before. Indeed, she said that as responder when I repeated any suit I had to have six of them. Could you please clarify this simple thing?

Caroline Vear of Melbourne, Australia

Answer: The bidding has been 1◇ : 1♠, 2♣ : 2♠. The expectation for 2♠ is 6+ spades or a very strong 5-card suit (including three honours). The reasons for this approach are:

1. Opener has shown nine cards in the two suits bid and so is unlikely to have 3-card support for just a 5-carder.

2. With only a 5-card suit yourself chances are strong that you will have support for one of opener's suits.

As 2♣ is not forcing you can pass with 3+ clubs or revert to diamonds with 2-3 diamonds. It will almost always be better to support one of opener's suits than to repeat a 5-carder. If opener does have 3-card support for your 5-carder, opener should have a strong hand. Why is that? Look at this hand:

♠ K 7 6
♡ 5
◇ A Q 8 4 3
♣ K 9 7 2

With this hand after 1◇ : 1♠, you should raise to 2♠ rather than bid 2♣.

♠ K 7 6
♡ 5
◇ A K 8 4 3
♣ A Q 7 2

With this hand after 1◇ : 1♠, bid 2♣, intending to show the spade support next time (if there is a next time).

After 1◇ : 1♠, 2♣ : 2♠ opener is expected to pass with a weak hand with a singleton or doubleton spade. That means it is sensible for responder to have six spades or a very strong 5-card suit to rebid the spades. Still, you may occasionally be stuck with a 5-5 pattern:

♠ Q J 5 4 3
♡ A 8 7 4 3
◇ 6
♣ 3 2

After 1◇ : 1♠, 2♣ a rebid of 2♠ here is the least of evils. The hand is too weak for 2NT or a forcing 2♡.

When responder rebids the same suit it is certainly a 6-card suit most of the time. For example, 1◇ : 1♡, 1♠ : 2♡ = six. 1♡ : 2♣, 2◇ : 3♣ = six and jump-rebids by responder in the same suit = six.

Dear Ron,

You are third to speak after two passes with both sides vulnerable in a crucial phase of a teams match and hold:

♠ A 9 8 6 5 3
♡ A Q 6
◇ A K
♣ 7 6

You open 1♠ and partner responds 2◇, which in your methods guarantees 10+ points or a strong rebiddable suit with 9+ points. What now?

Answer: Bid 3♠, despite the lack of suit quality, unless playing a 2-over-1 system where 2♠ would be forcing.

Continuing: My (Life Master) partner said it was clear that I had to manufacture a bid of 3♣. Was he correct?

Answer: I could understand manufacturing a bid of 2♡, where you have strength, and take the risk of partner having 4-card support there. To bid 3♣ is a psychic bid, hoping to finish in 3NT and ward off a club lead, but it could land the partnership in deep trouble if responder has length in clubs. 3♣ would attract very few votes from an expert bidding panel, where the popular action is likely to be 2♡ (forcing).

Continuing: In fact I chose to take the bull by the horns (be decisive) and bid 4♠.

T.G. of England

Wow! That would not be high on anyone's choice of action with a suit of this quality. Even 3♠ would be lambasted by some on that basis. Given that the jump to 3♠ is forcing after a 2-over-1 response, there is no need to jump to 4♠. That should suggest a weaker hand but better spades, say:

♠ A Q J 10 8 4 3
♡ A 7 6
♢ Q 2
♣ 5

Follow-up: We were not playing the 2-over-1 system or any variation of it. Partner held:
♠ Q
♡ K 10 9
♢ Q J 10 7 4 3 2
♣ Q 3

It would be interesting to know how you think the auction would go after your principal recommendation of 3♠ and after your alternative suggestion of 2♡. T.G.

Answer: For the 3♠ rebid, 1♠ : 2♢, 3♠, 4♢, 5♢ or for the 2♡ rebid, 1♠ : 2♢, 2♡ : 3♢, 4♢ (forcing) : 5♢. The lack of club control in either hand means that neither can presume to bid to slam. It is hard to see what 1♠ : 2♡, 3♣ would achieve except the possibility that you play 3NT and avoid a club lead. That risk might be fine at pairs, but at teams you do not want to take that chance when 5♢ is laydown. Raising a minor suit to the 4-level, as in 4♢ above, should be played as forcing and not invitational.

Dear Ron,
I've been puzzling over one facet of this deal from your bridge column (see opposite page). *This was West's 3NT reply to East's 3♣, fourth-suit-forcing. To me, 3NT promises a cover in clubs. Can you please explain where I am misunderstanding this convention?*
Louise Kobler of Sydney, Australia

Dealer West : North-South vulnerable

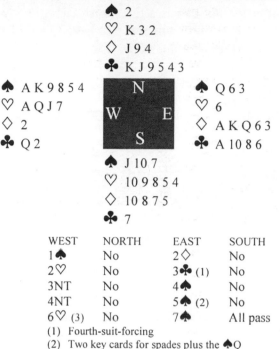

♠ 2
♡ K 3 2
◇ J 9 4
♣ K J 9 5 4 3

♠ A K 9 8 5 4
♡ A Q J 7
◇ 2
♣ Q 2

♠ Q 6 3
♡ 6
◇ A K Q 6 3
♣ A 10 8 6

♠ J 10 7
♡ 10 9 8 5 4
◇ 10 8 7 5
♣ 7

WEST	NORTH	EAST	SOUTH
1♠	No	2◇	No
2♡	No	3♣ (1)	No
3NT	No	4♠	No
4NT	No	5♠ (2)	No
6♡ (3)	No	7♠	All pass

(1) Fourth-suit-forcing
(2) Two key cards for spades plus the ♠Q
(3) Asking bid in hearts, grand slam try

The column continued: 'Using fourth suit to reach game (as opposed to 4♠ over 2♡) showed slam interest with 3-card support for opener. West had more than enough to become enthused. 6♡ asked East to bid the grand slam if holding the ♡K. East judged that her singleton heart plus diamond strength would be enough to take care of West's heart losers.'

Answer: Most top players will treat Q-x as a stopper in reply to fourth-suit-forcing. That allows partner to use fourth-suit with holdings like K-x-x, A-x-x or J-x-x, opposite which Q-x will be a useful holding.

33

It is true that if the fourth-suit bidder has x-x-x, then Q-x will not be effective but that is a risk worth taking. I say to my partners, 'If I bid fourth-suit and you have Q-x, bid no-trumps. If it goes wrong, I will take the blame.'

Ron,
Teams, both vulnerable.

West	East	*The bidding goes:*	
♠ A 9 4	♠ K J 8 7 3	West	East
♡ K	♡ J 7 6 4	1◇	1♠
◇ A 10 8 7 4	◇ J	3♣	3NT
♣ A Q 8 7	♣ 9 5 3	No	

Of course they attack hearts and I'm lucky to go only one off. At the other table, 4♠ was also one off. Partner would have liked me to rebid 3♠. What do you think of the whole auction?
George Biro of Sydney, Australia

Answer: Is it possible for partner to have 3-card spade support for the jump to 3♣? Surely. If so, partner will have a singleton or a void in hearts and then 3NT is unlikely to be the best spot.

3♠ suggests six spades or a very good five-card suit, enough for doubleton support. Why not 3♡, fourth-suit? That will buy you 4♠ with 3-card support, 3♠ with only a doubleton, 3NT with something in hearts (Q-x or better). If partner cannot do any of those, maybe 5♣ is best if partner happens to be 5-5.

Post script: The jump-shift to 3♣, forcing to game, is also worth a look. With 17 HCP including a singleton king, it would be enough to rebid 2♣. It is true that this may end the bidding, but if partner cannot muster another bid, so be it.

Two similar questions were received on standard American bidding concerning opener's 2NT rebid:

Dear Ron,

I really have a problem with the no-trump rebids. Please tell me how you would teach inexperienced players to rebid as opener with a 5-3-3-2 pattern after, say, 1 ♡ : 2♣.

Lynn Kalmin of Sydney, Australia

Ron,

Playing 'Standard' (say, 15-17 1NT), can you tell me what is the most common treatment among experts for the 2NT rebid after a 2-over-1 response? I've read in a few American books where they regard the bid as minimum (12-14) whereas I've always played it as extra values (15-18).

N.H. of Australia

Answer: There are two basic approaches:

1. Treat 5-3-3-2s with a 5-card major the same as a 5-3-3-2 with a minor and so open 1NT with 15-17, 15-18, 16-18, whatever the range is. Then a 2NT rebid after a 2-over-1 response can be 12-14 and a 3NT rebid 18/19-20.

2. If opening 1NT with a 5-card major is not the popular approach, then:

● Repeat the major if minimum
● Rebid 2NT with 15-18
● Rebid 3NT with 19-20

I normally teach this method, although I prefer playing that a 1NT opening can have a 5-card major. Many 5-card major players firmly believe that the two-level rebid of the major shows six. That is not correct and you simply need to give a couple of examples:

(a) ♠ A J 8 7 4　　　(b) ♠ A J 8 7 4
　　♡ 6　　　　　　　　　♡ 3 2
　　◇ A Q 9 8 2　　　　　◇ A K 7 5 2
　　♣ J 6　　　　　　　　♣ 2

In each case you open 1♠. If partner responds 2♣, no problem. You rebid 2◇. Then you ask, what if the response is 2♡? You are much too weak for 3◇, forcing to game, and not close to the shape for a natural 2NT. That means you have to rebid 2♠. *The function of repeating your suit after a two-level response is to show a minimum hand, not to promise an extra card in that suit.* Once you have received agreement on the above hands that a minimum 2♠ rebid is necessary, the logic of using the rebid of the major to show a minimum opening hand is not difficult.

♠ A 5 ♡ A K J 5 4 ◇ Q 3 2 ♣ A J 4	After 1♡ : 2♣ or 2◇, rebid 3NT. After 1♡ : 1♠, rebid 3NT.

♠ A 5 ♡ A K J 5 4 ◇ Q 3 2 ♣ Q J 4	After 1♡ : 2♣ or 2◇, rebid 2NT. After 1♡ : 1♠, rebid 2NT.

♠ A 5 ♡ A K J 5 4 ◇ Q 3 2 ♣ J 5 4	After 1♡ : 2♣ or 2◇, rebid 2NT. After 1♡ : 1♠, rebid 1NT.

♠ A 5 ♡ A K J 5 4 ◇ J 3 2 ♣ 8 6 5	After 1♡ : 2♣ or 2◇, rebid 2♡. After 1♡ : 1♠, rebid 1NT (standard American).

Chapter 5: Problems after a 2♣ opening

The most common advice sought after a 2♣ opening is how to handle a 4-4-4-1 pattern either as opener or as responder.

Dear Ron,
(a) In an uncontested auction, 2♣ : 2◇, 2♡ : 2♠ is it best to use 2♠ as a 4-card suit or as a cue-bid with heart support? Does support mean 3+ cards?
(b) If the auction started 2♣ : 2NT, 3♡ : 3♠, would 3♠ be a cue agreeing hearts?

George Biro of Sydney, Australia

Answer (a): It is best to use 2♠ as natural and a 5+ suit. With four spades only, no 5+ suit and no support for hearts, bid 2NT. You will not miss a 4-4 spade fit as opener can rebid 3♠ with four spades.

After 2♣ : 2◇, 2♡ three trumps would do to support hearts (as opener is expected to have 5+ hearts), as long as no more attractive action is warranted. It would be all right to rebid 2NT with 3-card heart support, intending to revert to hearts if opener's next bid does not suggest a better contract.

Answer (b): Yes. Once you have bid no-trumps and promised a balanced hand, a new suit is taken as a cue-bid with support for the last suit mentioned by partner. The same would apply in this sequence, 2♣ : 2◇, 2♡ : 2NT, 3♠ : 4♣ / 4◇. Responder's 4♣ / 4◇ should be taken as a cue-bid with support for spades. As responder can be weak here, it would be sensible for the cue-bid to be first- or second-round control.

Hi, Ron,

Here's a hand dealt at our local club that stumped everyone (including me)! We play weak twos in the majors, and use Benjamin Twos for strong openers. Can you tell us how you would have bid this hand?

♠ 5
♡ A K 8 2
♢ A Q 9 2
♣ A K Q 3

If you open with a strong two, partner will give a negative response. What would you do then? Would you open at the one-level? Partner's hand was:

♠ J 10 7
♡ J 9 6 5
♢ J 10 4
♣ 7 6 4

Carol Glen of Nelson, New Zealand

Answer: It is not surprising that so many were stumped. It is a very tough hand, indeed. I would not open at the one-level. That runs too great a risk of missing game. To open 2♣ Benjamin has the advantage that after 2♣ : 2♢, I can bid 2♡ cheaply, but the 2♡ rebid is not forcing and I might play it there. It is true that there is no guarantee that game is available for us, but you cannot wait for guarantees. With just three losers you should be prepared to commit to game.

I do not like the style where 2♣ : 2♢, 2NT or 2♢ : 2♡, 2NT is bid with a singleton. That is also risky. On the actual hand it would work out all right. 2♢ : 2♡, 2NT = 23-24 points, balanced (in theory). Then with 2+ points responder will kick on, bidding 3♣ Stayman or similar. Opener shows the hearts and responder raises to 4♡.

With 23 HCP and a shapely hand as opener, you should insist on game. As a general philosophy, if not sure where to go, aim high rather than low. Think what might go right rather than what could go wrong. So:

Opener	Responder
2♦	2♡
3♣	3NT (responder's likely rebid)
4♡	No

Responder will expect opener to have 5+ clubs, 4+ hearts, and the actual hand is not far off that. Some days this sequence will put you into 5♣. Maybe that will be the best spot. If not, accept that you cannot win them all.

If playing 2♣ as your game-force, opener should rebid 2♡:

Opener	Responder
2♣	2♦
2♡	4♡
No	

Opener's 2♡ rebid would be taken as forcing to game with 5+ hearts, while responder's 4♡ shows heart support but a very weak hand, weaker than a raise to 3♡.

Dear Mr Klinger,

My partner and I are slightly nonplussed by what you write in 'Bridge Conventions, Defences and Countermeasures' about the responses to a 2♣ (strong) opening bid. I quote from page 17, seventh paragraph:

'The 2NT response is used for balanced hands and suit responses should be taken as a 5-card major or longer suit. With 4-4-4-1 and positive values, bid 2♡ or 2♠, the cheaper 4-card suit, and do not worry. Most of the time it will not be critical that partner expects you to have five cards there.'

Answer: The 4-4-4-1 pattern is a problem in responding to a 2♣ opening. It is not attractive to treat it as balanced and it would usually be preferable to have the stronger hand declarer in no-trumps.

(continuing) As I understand this, the 2NT response is only for use on balanced hands, i.e., no worse than 5-3-3-2.

Answer: Normally only 4-3-3-3 or 4-4-3-2. With a 5-3-3-2 you can bid your 5-card suit unless the suit is weak.

(continuing) My partner interprets it that 2NT can be given on 4-4-4-1 hands, and that any response in a suit shows five cards minimum in that suit.

Answer: One can play that way, but that is not recommended.

(continuing) I believe that the suggestions you have made make it wrong to bid 2NT on a 4-4-4-1 hand,

Answer: Yes, it is undesirable.

(continuing) and therefore it is permissible to bid a four card suit; but your paragraph says that a four-card suit is to be bid only with 'positive values'. With a negative response, my partner believes we should bid as follows:

Opener   Responder
  2♣   2♢
  2♡ (say)   2♠ (say)
  The 2♠ bid is unconditionally a five-card suit; whilst my interpretation is that 2♠ could possibly be four cards only, if the hand pattern is 4-1-4-4.

Answer: If partner has bid your singleton, the 2NT rebid does not lack appeal. If opener has five hearts and four spades, opener can bid 3♠ over your 2NT rebid.

(continuing) My partner does not believe you mean this, and thinks that without a five-card suit, the response bid in the 2♠ position (above) should be 2NT.

Answer: I would go along with that.

In opposition to this, I think the 2NT bid is precluded by your statement that 'The 2NT response is used for balanced hands . . .'

Answer: The 2NT response is not the same as a 2NT rebid.

(continuing) Your guidance on this would be gratefully received, for the peace of mind of both of us!

John Williams of England

Answer: An attractive option when holding a 4-4-4-1 with positive values in response to a strong 2♣ opening is always to bid 2◇ and try to catch up later. That is why many now play 2♣ : 2◇ = negative or waiting. Similarly, if using Benjamin Twos, 2◇ : 2♡ can be negative or waiting. If adopting this approach, the 2NT response would always be balanced and a suit response would always be a 5+ suit.

If the bidding starts 2♣ : 2◇, 2♡ or 2♣ : 2◇, 2♠ you could then make a splinter jump with 4-card support and a singleton or rebid 2NT with the singleton in partner's suit and await further information from partner.

For example, 2♣ : 2◇, 2♠ : 2NT, 3NT : 4NT would say 'I am stronger than you could possibly expect from my 2◇ response . . .' while 5NT over 3NT would say, 'Pick a slam somewhere' or 6NT would show slam values with no 5+ suit and no fit for partner, hence a 4-4-4-1. It would make no sense for a genuine negative response to bid 4NT, 5NT or 6NT over 3NT in the given auction.

This query focuses on a problem similar to the preceding:

Dear Mr. Klinger,
 My partner and I play standard Acol with the addition of a Multi-2 ◇. Recently I was dealt the following hand:

♠ K
♡ A Q 9 3
◇ A K J 2
♣ K Q 10 5

I did not fancy 2NT with a 1-4-4-4 pattern. I considered the hand too strong for a 1-opening, but not strong enough for a 2 ♣ opening. That left little choice but to open 2-of-a-suit. I opened 2 ♡ and as partner had all the right cards, we ended in 6 ♡, making all thirteen tricks.

 My partner criticized the 2 ♡ opening for two reasons:
(a) My hand does not have eight playing tricks with hearts as trumps, and
(b) I did not have five or more cards in hearts.

 Partner's view is that I should have shaded the point count requirement and opened 2 ♣. My specific questions are:
(1) What is the correct opening bid with the above hand?
(2) Would an opening bid of 2 ♣ be better than 2 ♡?
(3) Is it absolutely necessary to have a long, strong suit with at least eight playing tricks in order to open two-of-a-suit?
(4) Could you suggest a possible bidding sequence, my partner's hand being:

♠ A 8 7 6
♡ K J 10 8 5
◇ Q 10 8 4
♣ - - -

(Name withheld)

Answer: In order of preference, choose a 1-opening, 2NT or open 2♣. The ♠K is a doubtful value and partner will strive to respond to a 1-opening. If partner does pass, perhaps fourth player will bid. If your 1-opening is passed out, perhaps game is not on.

While the shape is not ideal, it is closer to a 2NT opening than an Acol Two. The strength is not quite up to a 2♣ opening, which only delays the problem. What will you do after 2♣ : 2♢? Still, 2♣ is better than a 2♡ opening, which does show a long suit and 8+ playing tricks.

Here are two possible sequences:

Opener	Responder
1♢	1♡
3♠ (1)	4♣ (2)
4♢ (2)	4♠ (2)
4NT (3)	6♡ (4)
7♡	No

(1) Splinter, game-force, 4+ hearts
(2) Cue-bids
(3) Roman Key Card Blackwood
(4) Two key cards plus a useful void

Opener	Responder
1♢	1♡
3♠ (1)	5♣ (2)
5NT (3)	6♢ (4)
6NT (5)	7♡

(1) Splinter
(2) Lackwood/voidwood: Asking for key cards outside clubs
(3) Two key cards plus the ♡Q
(4) Asking in diamonds
(5) Shows the ♢K, no ♢Q

Details about slam asking bids and Lackwood can be found in *Bridge Conventions, Defences and Countermeasures.*

Hi, Ron,

Just home from a teams event. I was East, the dealer, with only the opponents vulnerable. These were my cards:

♠ K Q J 10 3 2
♡ A K Q 5 3
◇ 9
♣ A

I opened 2♣, no bid on my left and partner bid 2♡. North jumped to 5◇. What do you bid?

John Milston of Sydney, Australia

Answer: If 2♡ is a positive reply with hearts, I bid 6♡. There is a case for 6♠. A spade lead against 6♡ could see it fail. On the other hand there could be a heart ruff against 6♠. What happened?

Reply: 2 ♡ *was a positive. We use 2 ◇ as the negative. I bid 6 ♡. Partner had 8 points, but the player on lead had both missing aces and I went one down. I was criticised (mainly by the opponents*), but I thought that, percentage-wise, partner would have at least one ace, especially as he had a maximum of only one point in hearts.*

Answer: Yes, the odds are that partner has an ace and the danger is that partner has two aces and you make seven. Partner having no aces is the least likely scenario. Don't worry about this result. Next time it happens, bid 6♡ again.

---

*How gross! Players should learn how to behave properly. One never criticises one's partner, ones team-mates and certainly not an opponent.

Chapter 6: Questions on the Losing Trick Count

The Losing Trick Count* is an excellent hand valuation tool when your side has a decent trump fit and is more accurate than point count. To use the LTC, count your losers in the first three cards in each suit (the ace, king and queen are winners, lower cards are losers). Add your losers to the number shown by partner (take a minimum opening hand of around 13-15 points to be 7 losers, weaker hands have more losers, stronger hands have fewer losers). Subtract the total of your losers plus partner's from 24. The answer is the number of tricks your side is likely to take in your trump contract.

1. Teams, Dealer East : Game all	*What should East do with:*
West North East South	♠ Q 9 8 6
1◇ No	♡ K J 10 6
1♠ No ?	◇ A Q J 6
(See pages 46-47)	♣ K

2. Teams, Dealer West : Game all	*East's action with:*
West North East South	♠ A J 9 4
1♠ No ?	♡ A 7 4 3
(See pages 47-48)	◇ K Q 5 4 3
	♣ - - -

3. Teams, Dealer West : Game all	Suppose in #2 you bid 4♣,
West North East South	a splinter bid, showing the
1♠ No 4♣ (1) No	values for game, 4+ spades
4♠ No ?	and a club singleton or void.
(1) Splinter raise of spades	What next? *(see page 49)*

*For more information, see *The Modern Losing Trick Count*, published by Cassell in association with Peter Crawley in the Master Bridge Series.

Dear Ron,
Vulnerable at imps:

My partner held:	*My hand:*
♠ K 7 4 2	♠ Q 9 8 6
♡ A 9	♡ K J 10 6
◇ 9 2	◇ A Q J 6
♣ J 9 8 6 2	♣ K

The bidding went 1 ◇ : 1 ♠. I raised to 2 ♠, all pass.

I valued my hand as 6½ losers, but did not add any other losers even though we had an 8-card fit, because of my ruffing values. Before I started using the LTC I would have treated my hand as worth 16 Pts (I value a singleton as 3 points when I have four trumps) and would have raised 1 ♠ to 3 ♠. In discussing this hand with my partner I suggested that she owed me another bid because she had an 8-loser hand and that my hand potentially could have had 6 losers.

We wound up with a poor result because on the lie of the cards 4 ♠ is cold regardless of the defence. Had we been going strictly by point count the auction would have been 1 ◇ : 1 ♠, 3 ♠ : 4 ♠. My other point about this hand was despite the possibility of too many losers, should I have pushed to game because of the vulnerability and imp scoring?

Arthur Schein of Sacramento, USA

Answer:
On a raw count, 6½ losers is fine, but even then you might bid 1 ◇ : 1 ♠, 3 ♠. However, there are a number of plus values:
    The ♡J-10, the ◇J, the singleton ♣K and even the ♠9-8 makes the suit better than Q-6-3-2 (since J-10 doubleton with an opponent now also holds the trumps losers to one). Compare the actual hand with this one, also 6½ losers:

♠ Q 6 3 2   ♡ K 8 4 3   ◇ A Q 7 3   ♣ 10

'How much better is my hand than it might be for the number of losers I have?' is a sensible approach.

Partner might have made a trial bid of 3♣ but this is less clear-cut (and a significantly more aggressive action) than raising 1♠ to 3♠. Bidding on with just 8 HCP would be unattractive if the partnership tends to raise a major suit response with only three trumps.

Reaching 4♠ is all right at Imps, particularly vulnerable, but most of the time there will be two trump losers and you will need the ◇K onside, plus quite a bit of work setting up one hand or the other. It is not such a great contract, even though it should be reached.

After 1◇ : 1♠, a jump raise to 3♠ is enough. Pushing to 4♠ over 1♠ on your values is not warranted.

Dear Ron,
This hand came up yesterday and centres around the LTC in slams.

WEST	EAST
♠ K Q 8 3 2	♠ A J 9 4
♡ J 9	♡ A 7 4 3
◇ 10 9	◇ K Q 5 4 3
♣ A K 8 4	♣ - - -

East has better than a 5-loser hand (I adjust for more aces than queens) while West has a 6-loser hand. Based upon the LTC, slam should be assured and a grand might be close, but looking at both hands you have no play (pretty much) with a heart lead. Now, it might be argued that it takes a heart lead to beat this slam, but in any event this is a slam you do not want to be in.

I was in 6♠ and the opening lead was the ♡K from K-Q-x. Is there some adjustment that can be made with a void? (assuming the partner knows there is a void). I have found that the LTC is less accurate in bidding slams (need a source of tricks), but this one has me scratching my head. Any thoughts or suggestions?

Barry Turner of Dallas, USA

Answer:

The LTC never claims a contract should be 'assured'. All that is claimed is that there is or might be potential for the number of tricks estimated by the LTC.

The lower the level, the more variables come into the play and so the LTC might be seen to be more accurate at game-level than at slam-level, but it works very well there, too, depending on how much you know about each other's hands from the bidding. The existence of a singleton or a void is of primary importance and hence the value of splinter bids to see whether there are wasted high cards opposite the shortage. The phenomenon known as 'duplication' refers to the reduction in value of high cards facing shortage.

With ◇x-x-x facing ◇A-K-Q and ♣ --- opposite ♣x-x-x, you have no losers. If you have ◇x-x-x facing ◇x-x-x and ♣ --- opposite ♣A-K-Q there are three losers for the same high card content and the same losing trick count.

The problem with your hand is the duplication in clubs with two winners almost totally wasted. Make the ♣K the ♡K and 6♠ is great. Make the ♣K the ♡K and the ♣A the ◇A and you have an easy 7♠, yet the HCP and LTC have not changed. The only difference is the location of the winners, so you can hardly blame the LTC for reaching this poor slam.

Splinters and cue-bidding will often locate the cards needed for a slam or reveal the duplication that can kill a slam. This would be a reasonable auction for the actual cards held:

WEST	EAST
♠ K Q 8 3 2	♠ A J 9 4
♡ J 9	♡ A 7 4 3
◇ 10 9	◇ K Q 5 4 3
♣ A K 8 4	♣ - - -

1♠	4♣ (splinter)
4♠	5♣ (cue-bid, void in clubs)
5♠	No

West signs off over 4♣ because the hand drops below opening values once the ♣K becomes a wasted card opposite the club singleton or void. When East shows a club void, the ♣A becomes wasted as well. East deduces at this point that partner lacks both the ◇A and ♡K and so gives up on slam.

Suppose the hands looked like this:

WEST	EAST
♠ K Q 8 3 2	♠ A J 9 4
♡ J 9	♡ A 7 4 3
◇ A 9	◇ K Q 5 4 3
♣ K 8 4 2	♣ - - -

1♠	4♣
4♠	5♣
5◇	5♡
5♠	6♠
No	

5◇ and 5♡ are cue-bids, showing first-round control in the suit bid. 6♠ is enough and East might have bid 6♠ over 5◇.

WEST	EAST
♠ K Q 8 3 2	♠ A J 9 4
♡ K 9	♡ A 7 4 3
◇ A 9	◇ K Q 5 4 3
♣ 8 7 6 4	♣ - - -

1♠	4♣
4◇	4♡
5♡	5NT
6♡	7♠
No	

4◇ and 4♡ are first-round cue-bids. 5♡ = second-round heart control but no second-round control in clubs or diamonds. 5NT asks for the trump holding and 6♡ shows two top honours in spades.*

Hi, Ron,
Imps, vulnerable, we held:

♠ K Q J 7 4	♠ 1 0 6 5
♡ K J 4	♡ A Q 9 7
◇ A K 10	◇ 9 8 6
♣ J 6	♣ Q 9 4

1♠	2♠
3♠	No

Even with adjusting for controls, opener had a 6-loser hand opposite a 9½-loser hand and so in theory game should not be bid here. At most tables it went 1♠ : 2♠, 4♠. I suppose one answer could be like most systems the LTC does not always work and at Imps vulnerable you must push for game.

Arthur Schein of Sacramento, USA

---

*For another approach to bidding after a splinter, see the 'scroll' method on page 81.

Answer: Like other methods, the LTC should be used with judgement. It is true that the LTC does not always produce the perfect answer, but here a 1♠ : 2♠, 4♠ auction should be found. One way to consider these situations is to see how much better your hand is than the minimum for the same losers.

Contrast these two hands:

    (a) ♠ K Q J 7 4   (b) ♠ K Q 8 7 4
        ♡ K J 4   ♡ K 6 4
        ◊ A K 10   ◊ A K 2
        ♣ J 6   ♣ 8 6

With (b) also a 6-loser hand, even 3♠ is in some jeopardy. Note how the ♠J solidifies the suit and the ♡J provides a certain discard for the third diamond. *The Modern Losing Trick Count* recommends treating K-J-x as a plus value and it is sensible to upgrade the hand also for a jack with two higher honours (as with the above spades). I suspect that the problem this time is not the LTC but hand valuation.

Ron,
   Playing 5-card majors, partner opened 1♠. I held:
       ♠ Q 10 5 3   ♡ 10   ◊ K 7 5 4   ♣ Q J 8 6
   Playing Bergen raises I responded 3◊ (10-12 points and 4+ support), with 8 HCP and 3 points for the heart shortage. LHO came in with 3♡. Partner bid 3♠, showing a minimum and this was passed out. We made ten tricks easily. Over half the field bid 4♠. Using limit raises I would have bid 3♠ and again that would have been passed out.
   One top-level player suggested my response should be 4♠, based on having seven losers (two in spades, one in hearts, two in diamonds and two in clubs). I thought the spade holding would count as three losers.

                         (Name withheld)

Answer: After 1♠ : (No) : 3◇ : (3♡), what is the distinction between passing and 3♠? This is worth discussing with your regular partner. One should be an emphatic sign-off and the other a mild invitation to game.

The loser count definitely does suggest that you should reach 4♠. You have 7 losers and expectancy for a minimum opening is also 7 losers. 7 + 7 = 14 and 24 – 14 = 10 tricks potential. In spades you have only two losers with the ace and king missing. Count suits headed by Q-10 or Q-J as two losers. You can also count Q-x-x-x in a long suit bid by partner as just two losers.

If you play limit raises, your hand is too strong for that. Playing Bergen you can bid 3◇ and still bid 4♠ over partner's 3♠ sign-off when your playing strength warrants that. On the actual auction you have a comfortable 4♠ rebid over 3♠ since your singleton is in the opposition's suit. A shortage in their suit is a greater plus value than usual. If your heart holding had been K-x-x-x your hand would have diminished in value.

Post script: Playing Bergen 1♡/1♠ : 3♣ = 6-9 HCP and 4+ support, while 1♡/1♠ : 3◇ = 10-12 HCP and 4+ support. With the given hand, 1♠ : 3♣ is fine (showing your high card strength accurately), as long as you intend to bid 4♠ over a 3♠ suggested sign-off from partner. Likewise, the limit raise strength for a Bergen 3◇ response will normally not have a singleton. If you do, you can still bid 3◇ initially, but you must raise partner's 3-major proposed sign-off to game. A hand with 4+ support and 10-12 HCP and a short suit will be worth a shot at game. Indeed many players start their game-forcing splinter responses from 10+ HCP.

Chapter 7: Worries in the slam zone

Questions on slam hands are very frequent. This is hardly surprising. As slam hands are relatively rare (you can expect to have twelve tricks available your way on about one deal in every twenty), players have less exposure and hence less experience in this area.

1. Teams, Dealer West : Game all				What should East do at this
West	North	East	South	*point with:*
No	No	1♣	3♡	♠ A 8 7 3 2
4♢	No	4♠	No	♡ - - -
5♢	No	?		♢ 3
(See page 60)				♣ A K Q J 6 4 2

2. Teams, Dealer West : Game all				*East's next move with:*
West	North	East	South	♠ J 6 2
2♡(1)	No	2NT (2)	No	♡ A 7 4 2
3♡(3)	No	?		♢ A K 6 2
(1) Weak two opening				♣ A 2
(2) Strong inquiry				
(3) Maximum weak two, moderate suit				
(See page 61)				

3. Teams, Dealer West : Game all				*West's next move with:*
West	North	East	South	♠ 7
1♢	No	1♡	No	♡ - - -
3♣	No	3NT	No	♢ K J 10 9 5 4
?				♣ A K Q 8 7 3
(See page 72)				

Dear Ron,
I was South on this board:

Dealer East : Game all

```
                    ♠ A 9 4
                    ♡ K 6 4
                    ◇ A 10 8 5 2
                    ♣ J 7
      ♠ 7 5 3            N            ♠ 8 6 2
      ♡ A 9 8 7      W       E        ♡ Q J 10 5 3 2
      ◇ J 9 3            S            ◇ 7 6
      ♣ 10 9 6                        ♣ 5 3
                    ♠ K Q J 10
                    ♡ - - -
                    ◇ K Q 4
                    ♣ A K Q 8 4 2
```

WEST	NORTH	EAST	SOUTH
		No	2♣
No	2NT	No	3♣
No	3◇	No	3♠
No	4NT (1)	No	5♠ (2)
No	6NT	All pass	

(1) Roman Key Card Blackwood with spades as trumps
(2) Two key cards plus the ♠Q

The 2NT response to 2♣ seemed logical with 11-12 HCP,
but if the response had been 2◇, we could have found 7◇
(7♣ also makes). The bidding might have gone:

WEST	NORTH	EAST	SOUTH
		No	2♣
No	2◇	No	3♣
No	3♠	No	4♡
No	5◇	No	7◇
No	No	No	

My queries: (1) Should a response to 2♣ show a 5-card suit first or the HCP first?
(2) The 2NT response seems to have killed off any cue-bidding, or did it?

(Name withheld)

Answer: It is very tough to reach 7◇ or the superior 7♣. The problem is locating North's two aces and to ensure that one of them is not the ♡A.

To comment meaningfully, I would need to know your system and in particular the meaning of the 2♣ opening (it is a game-force, I presume), the 2NT response (does it show 11-12 points balanced or any 11-12 points or could it also be 8-10 points balanced?), the 3♣ rebid (was that natural, showing clubs, or asking for majors, North's 3◇ (did that show diamonds or deny majors in reply to 3♣ Stayman?).

On the actual auction, 2NT is certainly a reasonable response. Normally one shows a 5-card suit ahead of a balanced hand, but here the diamonds are nothing special and with an honour in every suit and enough values for slam, the 2NT response is appealing.

I have trouble with your suggested auction. What does the 2◇ response show? Is it negative or positive or natural, showing diamonds? What about North's 3♠ rebid? If that is a cue-bid with club support, why would North bypass a 3◇ cue-bid? In any event, does 3♣ promise a 6+ suit? Mightn't South have only five clubs and if so, why would North be in a rush to support clubs? 4♡ is clearly a cue-bid, but what does 5◇ mean? How did South know from the auction that North actually had a diamond suit?

If North's response had been 3♦, it would not have been difficult to reach 7♦:

WEST	NORTH	EAST	SOUTH
		No	2♣
No	3♦	No	4♦
No	4♠	No	5NT
No	6♣	No	7♦
No	No	No	

With K-Q-x support and a source of tricks outside via the club suit, the raise to 4♦ is eminently reasonable. North bids 4♠ as a cue-bid, denying control in hearts. South now needs to know only whether North has the ♦A. The jump to 5NT asks, 'How many of the top three trumps do you have?' In reply, 6♣ shows one top trump (6♦ would show none) and South jumps to the grand slam. (Some might play 6♣ shows no top trump and 6♦ shows one.)

Another option, if available, would be 2♣ : 3♦, 4♥ as a void in hearts with diamond support and asking for key cards outside hearts. After the 5♣ reply showing two key cards but no ♦Q, South could again jump to 7♦.

After 2♣ : 2NT, showing a balanced positive, this auction would be sensible:

North	South	
	2♣	(1) Natural, 5+ clubs
2NT	3♣ (1)	(2) Natural, diamond suit
3♦ (2)	3♠ (3)	(3) Natural, 4 spades
3NT (4)	4♣ (5)	(4) No support for spades or clubs
4♦ (6)	4♥ (6)	(5) Sets clubs as trumps
4♠ (6)	7♣	(6) Cue-bids, with clubs agreed as trumps
No		

Dear Ron,
Would like your bidding advice how to reach 7♠ here:

West	East
♠ K Q 7 6 5	♠ A J 10 8 2
♡ A 9 4	♡ K Q 8 5 3 2
◇ A Q	◇ 9 6
♣ A K 2	♣ - - -

Our bidding went:

West	East
2NT	3♡
4♡	4♠
6♣	No

Partner's jump to 6♣ made me believe 7♠ was on, but without enough information, bidding 7♠ would have been an educated guess. I think partner got too excited too quickly. Using simple Blackwood 4NT : 5◇, 5NT : 6◇ would give partner enough info to bid 7♠. What do you think?

(Name withheld)

Answer: The sequence you suggest is reasonable, but usually the unlimited hand takes control of slam bidding rather than the hand whose strength is known. Playing transfers:

West	East	
2NT	3◇	(transfer to hearts)
3♡	3♠	(spades as well as hearts)
4♠	4NT	(Roman Key Card Blackwood)
5◇ (1)	5♡	(asks for the trump queen)
5NT (2)	7♠	
No		

(1) 1 or 4 key cards for spades, obviously four
(2) 'I have the ♠Q.'

West might bid 4♣ over 3♠ as a cue-bid with spade support.

Playing natural methods is tougher, but this is reasonable:

West	East
2NT	3♡ (natural)
4♡	4NT (simple Blackwood)
5♠	5NT
7♡	No

The 5NT rebid does not just ask for kings, but also shows grand slam interest and confirms that no key cards are missing. The West hand could not be better and, with a source of tricks via the spade suit, West should jump to 7♡. The grand slam in spades is superior, but that is hard to reach once hearts have been supported.

Dear Ron,
I wonder what the best bidding is for these hands.

West	East
♠ K 10	♠ Q J 5 2
♡ K Q 10 7 6 4	♡ A J
◇ - - -	◇ K J 6 2
♣ A 10 8 5 3	♣ Q J 6

The bidding was:

West	East
1♡	1♠
2♣	3♡
4♡	4NT (agreeing hearts)
5♡	No

Partner gave the wrong reply to RKCB and bid 5 ♡ instead of 5 ♠ to show two key cards for hearts plus the ♡Q. Is there a better way? Would it have been better to start 1 ♡ : 1 ♠, 2 ♣ : 2 ◇ (fourth-suit), 3 ♣? If so, what should I do next?

(Name withheld)

Answer: 6♡ or 6♣ is all right as a slam, but nothing special. You have to lose to the ♠A and the ♣K is missing. The slam thus depends on the club finesse and the chance of success is a bit under 50%. Really bad breaks might beat the slam even if the ♣K is onside. On the actual sequence it would be reasonable to pass 4♡.

If you start 1♡ : 1♠, 2♣ : 2◇ (fourth-suit, forcing to game), and opener rebids 3♣ (a jump to 4♣ would be sensible), responder has to decide whether to support hearts or clubs or try 3NT. It would be reasonable to bid 3NT, although there is some risk. A diamond lead to the ace and a diamond back might see 3NT fail.

At pairs, supporting hearts is attractive. If you do support hearts and partner bids only 4♡, I would leave it there. Your values in spades and diamonds are likely to be of little help opposite partner's maximum of three cards in those suits. If partner does make a slam move, you could jump to 6♣ to give partner a choice of slams. Partner would revert to 6♡.

Hi, Ron,
 Left-hand opponent opens 3♠, passed round to you. You hold:
♠ - - -
♡ A K 5
◇ K Q
♣ A K Q 8 7 5 3 2
Your bid, please?

Mick Aldridge of Northants, England

Make your own decision and then turn the page.

Answer to previous query: 6♣.

Hi, Ron,

West	East
♠ K Q	♠ A 8 7 3 2
♡ J 9 8 3	♡ - - -
◇ K Q 10 9 6 5	◇ 3
♣ 5	♣ A K Q J 6 4 2

The bidding went:

West	North	East	South
No	No	1♣	3♡
4◇	No	4♠	No
5◇	No	No	No

(a) Do you agree with West's initial pass?
(b) Do you agree with East's pass of 5 ◇

Eva of London, England

Answers: No. West is definitely worth a 1◇ opening (see page 10, where this problem was discussed).

(b) Bidding 6♣ over 5◇ is sensible. If partner could not open with 1◇, 3◇ or 4◇, then passing 5◇ is not reasonable when you hold a solid 7-card suit. Either partner's diamonds will not be solid or if they are, 6♣ should be a good chance.

You have not made 6♣ yet, of course, but it is a much better chance than 5◇. If a heart is led against 6♣, you ruff, draw trumps and play a diamond to the king. You can try to bring the diamond suit in with the residual chance that spades are 3-3. A spade lead would make it more awkward, as it is now more difficult to set up the diamonds. You could draw trumps and finesse the ◇10 or still play a diamond to the king and hope the ◇J falls or spades are 3-3.

60

Dear Ron,

Can you think of any legitimate sequence to the laydown small slam on the following pair of hands, please, with West opening with a weak 2 ♡:

West	East
♠ 5	♠ J 6 2
♡ K J 10 8 6 5	♡ A 7 4 2
◇ Q J	◇ A K 6 2
♣ K 9 6 3	♣ A 2

HJS77, bridge teacher, London, England

Answer: How about:

West	East
2♡	2NT (1)
3♡ (2)	4♣ (3)
5♣ (4)	5◇ (3)
5♠ (4)	6♡
No	

(1) Strong inquiry
(2) Maximum points, moderate suit (1 of top three honours)
(3) First-round cue-bid, hearts set as trumps
(4) Cue-bid showing second round control

In a partnership where the first cue-bid can be first- or second-round control, West would bid 4♠ over 4♣. East could then check on key cards with 4NT and bid 6♡ when West has one.

Some pairs use 2NT to ask for range and shortage. That would work here. In reply, 3♡ shows any minimum, 3NT = maximum, no shortage, while 3♣ / 3◇ / 3♠ = maximum and short in the suit bid. The auction would then commence 2♡ : 2NT, 3♠ (shortage and maximum) and that should be enough for East to continue with 4NT and bid 6♡ when West shows one key card.

Dear Ron,

These hands came up in one of my social games:

West	East
♠ A K Q 7 6 4	♠ 10 3 2
♡ K 8 5	♡ A J 6 3 2
◇ A J 8	◇ 7 6 5
♣ 9	♣ A K

The bidding:

West	East
2♣	2♡
2♠	3♠
4NT	5♡
5NT	6◇
6♠	No

Did I err in bidding 6♠ and not 7♠? The club lead allowed me to draw trumps, which were 2-2. Then all followed to ♡K, ♡A, but the ♡Q did not drop. A heart was discarded on dummy's second club and so all thirteen tricks were made. Would you therefore conclude that 7♠ was a worthwhile risk?

(Name withheld)

Answer: 6♠ is a sensible contract. 7♠ is a respectable grand slam, but is not warranted, even though you made all the tricks as the cards lay. It is true that on a diamond lead, chances are that you will make seven or go down in six, but without a diamond lead 6♠ is an excellent spot, while 7♠ would be a poor shot if an opponent held ♠J-x-x.

There is an interesting point in the play. What is the best line in 6♠?

If you receive a club lead, take the ace and test the trumps. If spades are 2-2, you can then play ♡K, heart to the ace and if hearts are 3-2, discard a heart on the second club winner and ruff the hearts good, as you did. This is your best chance for 13 tricks and you still make 12 tricks even if hearts are 4-1.

If North shows out on the second heart, duck it to South, win the diamond return with the ace and play a heart to the ace and ruff a heart. That leaves dummy with a heart and a club winner, so over to the ♠10 and discard your diamond losers on dummy's winners.

Finally, if North follows to the second heart on which you play the ♡A, and South shows out (meaning North still has ♡Q-x left), ruff your club winner to reach your hand and lead your third heart. Again the ♠10 will be the entry to reach the established heart winners.

Hi, Ron,
Which book would help me in my slam bidding? I am particularly interested in techniques that uncover mirror fits between the two hands.

Arthur Schein of Sacramento, USA

Answer: For that you need some relay system. One that would fit any 5-card major approach is *The Power System*, where the 2♢ response is an artificial game-force relay and you can then find opener's precise shape. You can hitch the Power 2♢ response to your current methods without adopting the rest of the Power system. Other relay systems exist, of course.

(continuing): Are there any techniques that enable you to locate queens other than the trump queen?

Answer: That is feasible by simple asking bids after the reply to Roman Key Card Blackwood. Once the trump queen has been shown or denied, then a bid in a non-trump suit can be used to ask for the king and queen of that suit (the ace will already be known from the RKCB answer). These new suit bids are called 'control asks' and in reply to a control ask:

Step 1 = no king, no queen
Step 2 = queen, no king
Step 3 = king, no queen
Step 4 = king + queen
Step 5 = king + queen + jack

If the location of the trump queen has not been revealed yet (after a 0/3 or a 1/4 reply to RKCB), then the cheapest non-trump bid asks for the trump queen and other non-trump suit bids are control asks, as above.

In replying to the trump queen ask, we use only Step 1 = no, Step 2 = yes, so that partner then has asking bids available in other suits. After the reply to the trump queen ask, a new suit is again a control ask.

(continuing): In 'Practical Slam Bidding' you advocate that the first cue-bid may be first- or second-round control, but in 'Cue-Bidding To Slams' the first cue-bid shows either the ace or a void in that suit.

Answer: 'Cue-Bidding to Slams' has the standard approach of cue-bidding aces and voids before kings and singletons. 'Practical Slam Bidding' encourages a superior approach in showing first- or second-round controls on the first round of cue-bidding. One advantage occurs when you bypass a suit and thus deny first- and second-round control in that suit. That may keep you lower more quickly.

(continuing): I have also been told never to initiate a Blackwood sequence when holding a worthless doubleton. Is that correct?

Answer: In general that is sound advice. With a worthless doubleton one usually starts with a cue-bidding auction. That will discover whether partner has control in the unguarded suit. One cannot always do this and sometimes one just has to take the risk. Sometimes you know the partnership has so many points that it is almost certain partner has the danger suit controlled.

(continuing): What I have been doing when holding two small is to jump in that suit to the five-level, which asks partner whether he has first- or second-round control of that suit.

Answer: That would be appropriate if that were your sole concern and you had enough knowledge about the aces, top trumps and had every other suit controlled.

(continuing): Perhaps you can suggest a better method of handling this situation.

Answer: See above, using cue-bidding.

(continuing): If the first cue-bid is made with a king, how can partner tell it is not the ace or a void that is being shown?

Answer: Partner does not know at the point when the cue-bid is made. In this style of cue-bidding, first make sure that the values for slam exist and that you have an agreed trump suit. Cue-bidding then ensures the partnership has first- or second-round control in every suit outside trumps (if not, sign off). Then use RKCB to check on aces and the top trumps.

Hello, Ron,

Could you comment on the bidding of this deal, which I witnessed last night?

Dealer East : East-West vulnerable

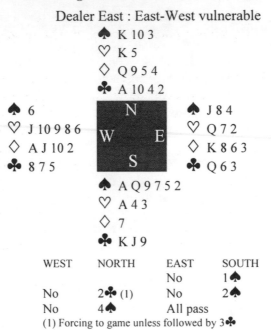

♠ K 10 3
♡ K 5
◇ Q 9 5 4
♣ A 10 4 2

♠ 6
♡ J 10 9 8 6
◇ A J 10 2
♣ 8 7 5

♠ J 8 4
♡ Q 7 2
◇ K 8 6 3
♣ Q 6 3

♠ A Q 9 7 5 2
♡ A 4 3
◇ 7
♣ K J 9

WEST	NORTH	EAST	SOUTH
		No	1♠
No	2♣ (1)	No	2♠
No	4♠	All pass	

(1) Forcing to game unless followed by 3♣

I don't like the auction at all, since I feel that North's 2♣ bid focuses on the club suit too strongly.

Answer: What response should North give? A Jacoby 2NT game-force with spade support promises 4+ trumps. If you disagree with a certain action, you need to provide some better choice.

(continuing): Can you comment on South's final pass in relation to the Losing Trick Count?

Answer: South had virtually no option other than to pass 4♠. North has shown no slam interest and the five-level is not necessarily safe. Interchange North's red suits to see why.

(continuing): I'm thinking that North is showing 6-7 losers and, together with South's 6-loser hand, it should be safe to try for slam.

Answer: North's 4♠ should be 7 losers (or worse) and North in fact has 7½ losers, counting the diamonds as 2½ losers, not two, because of the unsupported queen. Further, North would not be aware that South has six losers rather than seven. The hands fit well, but even so slam is nothing special, since it relies on no loser in clubs. That puts it around the 50% mark.

(continuing): Also, South's first- or second-round control of all suits and the bolstering of the club holding after North's 2♣ bid makes slam a worthwhile prospect. Slam would be very good opposite a perfect minimum holding of:

♠ K x x   ♡ x x x   ◇ x x   ♣ A Q x x x

and so passing 4♠ is much too timid.

(Name withheld)

Answer: Both North and South could have done more, but it is no shame to miss this slam.

(a) Assuming South's 2♠ rebid promised six spades, North might have bid 3♠ (strong) rather than 4♠ (weaker) to give South a chance to express slam interest with a cue-bid.

(b) In a natural system South might have jumped to 3♠ over 2♣ (definitely if 2♠ could be passed), but as 2♣ was almost game-forcing, there was no need to jump to 3♠, which is usually reserved for a stronger suit than the one South had.

With no jump to 3♠ available, South's 2♠ forcing could be even stronger than this and so with 3-card support North should encourage with 3♠ rather than jump to 4♠. If North had ♠K-x only, 6♠ would be a poor bet, requiring both spades to break and no club loser.

(c) South could have insisted on game and shown the club support by bidding 3♣ over 2♣. North should then bid 3♠ (strong) and start the slam ball rolling. That would lead to an excellent slam if South's clubs were just a touch stronger, say, ♣K-Q-x.

Dear Ron,
Playing match-points:

West	East
♠ A 6	♠ K
♡ A K Q 5	♡ J 9 3 2
◇ 8 6 2	◇ A K 5 4
♣ J 10 4 3	♣ A Q 9 6

The bidding:

	West	East
	1♣	1◇
	1♡	4NT
	5♠ (1)	6♡
	No	

(1) Two key cards + the ♡Q

As East I evaluated my hand as 5½ losers and assigned my partner no more than 7 losers for her opening bid. Do you agree with the evaluation and the bidding sequence?

Arthur Schein of Sacramento, USA

Answer: The East hand has six losers. The slam is reasonable, on the club finesse, but not great. Take away the ♣J or ♣10 and the slam is very poor. (Also, West has three key cards.)

Possible sequences:

West	East
1♣	1♦
1♡	3♠ (splinter)

The 3♠ splinter is reasonable despite the singleton king, since if partner has too much wasted in spades, there might be less available in the minor suits. After 3♠, abide by partner's decision.

West	East
1♣	1♦
1♡	1♠ or 2♠, whichever is fourth-suit.

Then over 1NT (or 2NT over 2♠) jump to 4♡ to show a hand stronger than 1♣ : 1♦, 1♡ : 4♡. Again abide by whatever partner decides next. I would not be upset about missing this slam, especially not at match-points.

(continuing): Playing match-points:

West	East
♠ A K J 2	♠ Q 10 8 4
♡ A 8	♡ K 10 4
♦ 6 5	♦ K 9 8
♣ A Q J 10 6	♣ K 8 7

The bidding:

West	East
1♣	1♠
4♠	4NT
5♣ (1)	6♠
No	

(1) 1 or 4 key cards for spades

We made 6♠, a slam reached by only four other pairs. Do you agree with the bidding?

Answer: Yes.

(continuing): I evaluated my hand (East) as 8 raw losers, but upgraded it because of my three cover cards. Should I have added half a loser to my hand for each missing ace, plus another half for only an eight-card trump fit?

Answer: No. Counting eight losers for East is a sound assessment. Any deficiency through lack of aces is counter-balanced by the fit with clubs.

Hi, Ron,
  How would you bid these hands to get to the slam? Most played it in 3NT. Could you suggest methods (a) using fourth-suit-forcing and (b) not using fourth-suit-forcing.

West	East
♠ K 9 5 2	♠ A 7 6
♡ K	♡ A 9 4 3 2
♢ K 8 6 3 2	♢ A Q 10
♣ A K 5	♣ Q 8

West opens 1 ♢. No opposition bidding.

(Name withheld)

Answer (a): With fourth-suit forcing to game:

West	East	
1 ♢	1 ♡	
1 ♠	2 ♣	(fourth-suit)
2NT	3 ♢	
4NT	5 ♣	(0 or 3 key cards, obviously 3)
5 ♡	5NT	(shows the trump queen)
6 ♣	6 ♡	(shows the ♣Q)
6NT	No	

4NT is Roman Key Card Blackwood, 5♡ asks for the trump queen and 6♣ is a control ask in clubs (see page 64). After discovering all this information, West has to decide whether to play in 6◇ or 6NT. West can count on seven tricks outside diamonds. If the diamonds behave there are twelve tricks in either contract. There is also a good chance that East supported diamonds with four trumps.

The safer slam is 6◇ as you might succeed there even with a trump loser. If you have a loser in diamonds, 6NT is in severe jeopardy. If you judged that the field is not strong, you might choose 6◇ rather than 6NT. In a strong field where most of the pairs with a combined 32 count will find slam, you would want to take your chances on the diamonds behaving and play in 6NT. 7◇ might be on, but it is not worth the risk.

With fourth-suit forcing for one round:

West	East
1◇	1♡
1♠	2♣
3NT	4◇

then as per opposite page or East might just raise 3NT to 6NT.

Without using fourth-suit forcing:

West	East
1◇	1♡
1♠	3◇ . . .

I would expect the jump to 3◇ to be forcing if fourth-suit forcing is not available. West could then continue with 4NT, as opposite, depending on what slam methods are available for a pair who do not use fourth-suit.

71

Dear Ron,

Help! If the bidding on the hands below starts 1 ◇ : 1 ♡, 3 ♣ : 3NT, how should it continue?

West	East
♠ 7	♠ A 6 3
♡ - - -	♡ J 8 7 5
◇ K J 10 9 5 4	◇ A Q 7 6
♣ A K Q 8 7 3	♣ J 10

(Name withheld)

Answer: Suggested bidding:

West	East
1 ◇	1 ♡
3 ♣	3NT (1)
4 ♣	4 ◇
4 ♡ (2)	4 ♠ (2)
5NT (3)	7 ◇
No	

(1) See later. 3NT is not the recommended rebid.
(2) Cue-bid, first-round control
(3) Grand slam trump ask

West's 4 ♣ is forcing, showing slam interest. East's 4 ◇ agrees diamonds as trumps. After East cue-bids the ♠A, West uses 5NT to ask for East's trump holding. Some bid seven if holding two top honours. Others would bid 6 ♡ to show two top honours (and bid 6 ◇ with none, 6 ♣ with one and seven only with all three top trumps). To reach 7 ◇ would be a brilliant outcome. Even reaching 6 ◇ should be a good result as it is not straightforward to find the slam.

After 1 ◇ : 1 ♡, 3 ♣ East should not bid 3NT. Facing a jump-shift, East has values for slam with the excellent fit for diamonds. A jump to 4 ◇ would express that.

Chapter 8: Mentions of conventions

Hi, Ron,
(1) Can I use garbage Stayman with these cards:
  ♠ 8 5 4 3   ♡ 9 7 6 2   ♢ 8 6 3 2   ♣ 9
if we are playing Extended Stayman with a 15-18 1NT?

(2) Partner opened 1NT and I had this hand, playing pairs:
  ♠ K 10 8 6 2   ♡ 7 6 5 3 2   ♢ Q 6   ♣ 7
  What do you recommend, playing transfers?
        Dave Hurst, ex Wigan, now of Darwin, Australia

Explanation: 'Garbage Stayman' is the use of the 2♣ reply on a weak hand, intending to pass any rebid by opener. It is suitable for three-suited hands short in clubs when the only permissible rebids after 1NT : 2♣ are 2♢, 2♡ or 2♠ (in other words, when playing simple Stayman).

Playing 'Extended Stayman' the rebids after 1NT : 2♣ are at the two-level with a minimum hand and at the three-level with a maximum hand (with 3♢ showing both majors and 3♣ denying a major).

Answer: (1) No, when playing Extended Stayman, you cannot afford to bid 1NT : 2♣ with a rotten hand, as opener's rebid might be an unsuitable 3♣ or 2NT (no major suit). Even if you heard 3♢, maximum and both majors, bids of 3♡ or 3♠ are forcing and show slam interest, not sign-offs.

(2) If you play simple Stayman, you can bid 1NT : 2♣ and if you receive a major suit reply, raise to three to invite game.

If partner replies with 2♢, continue with 2♠. Most play this as a sign-off and partner should pass 2♠. If partner does bid 2NT over 2♠, then bid 3♡ as a mild game invitation. If 1NT : 2♣, 2♢ : 2♠ is invitational in your methods, that is mildly aggressive with these cards. You would not mind inviting game if opener has a 4-card major, but opposite only three trumps, chances for game are not nearly as good.

If 1NT : 2♣ is Extended Stayman and you merely wanted to sign-off, bid 1NT : 2♡, transfer, and pass a 2♠ rebid, but bid 4♠ over a super-accept. This is not perfect as 4♡ could be on, but Extended Stayman is unsuitable for weak hands. You would not want to be in game opposite a minimum 1NT and you have no safe escape after 1NT : 2♣, 2NT, which shows a minimum 1NT and no 4-card major.

Another option is 1NT : 2♣ as a puppet to 2♢*, followed by 2♠ to invite game. If opener bids 2NT, no spade fit, continue with 3♡, still inviting game and showing a 5-5 pattern.

Hi, Ron,
A problem with the Lebensohl Convention:
The opponents bid a natural 2♣ over partner's 1NT opening. Using double as takeout one cannot use the Lebensohl 2NT to promise a club stopper as the 2NT bid forces partner to bid 3♣ anyway.
So, how can we:
(a) Find out if partner has a 4-card major for a 4-4 fit?
(b) Show a stopper in clubs? I presume an immediate 3♣ would deny a stopper and show at least one major.
Mick Aldridge of Northants, England

---

*See Bid Better, Much Better After Opening 1NT, published by Cassell in association with Peter Crawley in the Master Bridge Series.

Explanation: The Lebensohl Convention is a bid of 2NT by responder after second player intervenes over a 1NT opening. Using this approach, a suit bid at the three-level is forcing, while 2NT (called a 'puppet bid') requires opener to bid 3♣. Responder might be intending to pass 3♣. If not, a new suit lower-ranking than the overcall is not forcing and is merely competing for the part-score. Bidding 3NT or the opposition suit after the 2NT puppet, or without using 2NT, carries information about unbid majors and whether a stopper is held in the enemy suit.

Answer: You could play that 3♣ denies a stopper and does not show or deny a major and that 2NT, forcing 3♣, followed by a major suit bid or 3NT promises a stopper, but there is a much better method.

Assuming that you think your methods after a 1NT opening are the best you can play, why should you lose them? The 2♣ overcall has not taken away any bidding space. The most sensible approach after 1NT : (2♣) is to play 'system on', with double being your normal use for 2♣ (Stayman or Puppet or Gladiator, or whatever you play), with 2♦ / 2♡ / 2♠ etc., as your normal transfer or other structure. After partner's reply to 2♣, you can rebid 3♣ to ask for a club stopper if that is your problem.

Ron,

I'm sure that in one of your books (maybe with a co-author) you recommended five to ten conventions which would serve most average bridge players well.

Answer: No, that sounds like a book by someone else.

*(continuing): I've reread the books, but cannot find that piece
again. With the rise of conventions, such as Jacoby 2NT etc.,
is there a current set you would recommend, what you would
currently consider / recommend as the best / most useful /
most often arising 5 to 10 conventions for today's bridge world.*

(Name withheld)

Answer: No problem. Also it is a question of what you
consider as a convention and how advanced you want to be.

Constructive auctions

1. 1NT : 2♣ and 2NT : 3♣ inquiries
2. Transfers after 1NT and 2NT
3. Jacoby 2NT
4. Fourth-suit forcing
5. Splinters
6. Roman Key Card Blackwood

Competitive bidding:

1. Negative, competitive, support and responsive doubles
2. Unusual 2NT and the Michaels Cue Bid
3. Pre-emptive jump raises of overcalls, combined with:
4. Bidding the enemy suit to show a strong raise

20 Great Conventions Flipper, containing methods which
are state of the art for the modern game, and *Bridge
Conventions, Defences and Countermeasures* describe these
methods and defences to them.

Hi, Ron,

Please advise the best auction for this pair of hands:

West	East
♠ 7 3	♠ K Q J 8 2
♡ Q 9 8 7 6 5	♡ 3
◇ A K	◇ 3
♣ 7 5 3	♣ A K Q 8 4 2

West opens 2♢, multi. We play a 2NT response as forcing for one round, unless there is a further change of suit, while any response at the three-level is regarded as a game-force. My view is that, with no opposition bidding, it should go:

West	East
2♢	3♣
3♡	3♠
4♣	4NT
5♣	No

Bill Turner of Bridgend, Wales

Answer: A reasonable auction might start:

West	East
2♢	3♣
3♡	3♠
3NT	4♠ ...

At pairs West should pass 4♠. East is very likely to make 4♠ as long as spades are not 5-1. On the probable diamond lead, East discards the heart loser and then leads trumps. With a singleton spade West would choose 5♣. With a doubleton spade, it is a reasonable to pass 4♠ at pairs.

After 3♠ West bids 3NT because of the strong diamonds. On a diamond lead 3NT should be easy unless clubs are 4-0.

At teams, 5♣ is likely to be safer than 4♠ and West should bid 5♣ over 4♠. The 3♣, then 3♠, then 4♠ sequence shows at least five spades and six clubs. It follows that East's spades must be strong as East is prepared to play a 5-2 fit.

In the auction above, 4NT is very, very dangerous. It is most unlikely that West has two aces and a 5♢ reply (whether 0 or 1 ace) would be calamitous. One reason East suggests 4♠ is that the partnership could be missing three aces.

Dear Ron,

Following your advice we use 5-card Puppet Stayman over 2NT. We have had trouble with slam potential responding hands showing at least 5-4 in the minors and with similar strength hands containing at least one 4 card major and at least 5+ cards in one minor. I appreciate that these hands do not occur that often, but twice in the last few months we have ended up returning a poor score-card to our team-mates because we got in a tangle.

What do you and other experts do, using 5-card Puppet Stayman? Accept that no system is perfect and take a punt? Consider using Modified Baron in which the 3♠ response to 2NT is freed up to cater for minor suit hands? Or (hopefully) have a systemic method that allows us to retain the benefits of 5-card Puppet Stayman whilst coping with the problem shapes mentioned above?

T.G. of England

Answer: After 2NT : 3♣ responder's rebid of 4♣ / 4◇ (sooner or later) can be used to show a 5-card suit with slam interest if no major fit has been found. So:

2NT : 3♣
3♡ : 4♣ / 4◇ = 5-card minor

2NT : 3♣
3♠ : 4♣ / 4◇ = 5-card minor

We play that
2NT : 3♣
3♡ : 3♠ = game-force, slam interest, support for hearts

2NT : 3♣
3♠ : 4♡ = game-force, slam interest, support for spades

Since we can show strong support for the 5-card major this way, the 4♣ / 4♦ rebids remain free to show a 5+ suit and slam interest.

2NT : 3♣
3♦ : 3♥ (4 spades)
3NT : 4♣ / 4♦ = 5+ suit, slam interest

2NT : 3♣
3♦ : 3♠ (4 hearts)
3NT : 4♣ / 4♦ = 5+ suit, slam interest

2NT : 3♣
3NT : 4♣ / 4♦ = 5+ suit, slam interest

With 4-4 / 5-4 / 4-5 / 5-5 in the minors, we do bid 2NT : 3♠ to show both minors and slam interest. Opener can then bid 4♣ / 4♦ with 4+ support, else 3NT. Over 3NT, responder can still rebid 4♣ / 4♦ to show a 5-card minor.

2NT : 5NT is used to force to slam and asks opener to 'pick a slam'. Opener bids a good 5-card suit or a powerful 4-card suit (K-Q-J-x or stronger). If this does not suit, responder can make another suggestion. If no trump fit comes to light, the partnership will finish in 6NT.

Dear Ron,

If 2NT : 3♠ is no longer used to show 5 spades - 4 hearts, how do you show that sort of hand under the new ideas you have outlined? Isn't 2NT : 3♥, 3♠ : 4♥ likely to show at least 5-5 in the majors?

T.G. of England

Answer: The expectation for 2NT : 3♡ (transfer), 3♠ : 4♡ would be 5-5 in the majors and no slam interest. Opener would pass or correct to 4♠.

With 5 spades – 4 hearts, one could simply transfer to spades and rebid 3NT. The loss occurs when opener is 2-4 in the majors, which is less frequent than opener having three spades. However, most of us would not want to miss even this fit or a possible 5-4 fit in hearts.

Therefore, a slightly more complex version of 2NT : 3♣ has been developed. There are a number of versions, but this one, created by my bridge partner, Bruce Neill, is as good as it gets. It does require a little extra learning and a fair bit of practice until players are used to it, but it covers the 5 spades – 4 hearts problem very well.

2NT : 3♣ = 'Do you have a 5-Major?'
3♡ / 3♠ = Yes
3◇ = no 5-major, either at least one 4-major or 3 spades
3NT = no 5-major, no 4-major, no three spades.

2NT : 3♣
3◇ : ?

    3♡ = no major or 4 spades (opener bids 3♠ with four spades or 3NT without four spades)

    3♠ = 4 hearts (opener bids 3NT without four hearts)

    3NT = 4-4 majors, no slam interest

    4NT = 4-4 majors with slam interest

    5NT = Pick a slam

    4♡ = 5 spades, 4 hearts, no slam interest

    4♠ = 5 spades, 4 hearts and slam interest. Forcing.

    4♣ / 4◇ can be used to show 4-4-4-1s with both majors, while 3♡ over 3◇, followed by 4♣ / 4◇ show the 5-card minor and slam interest.

Dear Ron,

My partner and I decided to adopt scrolling and were going to play it until we came up with a stumbling block, which neither of us can resolve. You said that signing off in the agreed suit is just that – a sign-off. How then does one progress the bidding when it goes 1♡ : 4◇? You said a relay is asking if partner has a singleton or a void, but 4♡ would now be a sign-off, wouldn't it?

Similarly with 1♠ : 4♡. Isn't 4♠ a sign-off now?

We were thinking, what if opener had opened light and had wasted values and now wanted to sign off in the agreed suit? Are we now on a runaway train and cannot sign off?

Louise Payne of England

Answer: (1) You can always sign off in the trump suit.
(2) After 1♡ : 4◇ (splinter), 4♡ = sign-off, 4♠ = scroll.
(3) After 1♠ : 4♡ (splinter), 4♠ − sign-off, 4NT = scroll

Explanation: After partner makes a splinter bid (or shows a singleton after a 2NT Jacoby response), the cheapest bid other than the trump-suit is 'scroll' (a method devised by George Smolanko of Australia), asking partner whether a singleton or a void is held. In reply, the cheapest bid = singleton (after which the next cheapest bid other than the trump suit asks for key cards), and higher bids show key cards and promise a void. For example, after 1♠ : 4♣ (splinter), 4◇ = scroll. Then:

4♡ = singleton club (over which 4♠ = sign-off and 4NT asks for key cards)
4♠ = club void and 0 or 3 key cards
4NT = club void and 1 or 4 key cards
5♣ = club void and 2 key cards, no trump queen
5◇ = club void, 2 key cards plus the trump queen

Dear Ron,

My partner and I are learning cue-bidding from your 'Cue-Bidding To Slams'. Recently we played this hand:

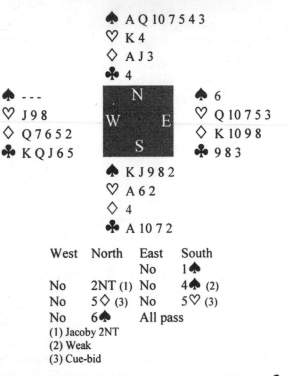

♠ A Q 10 7 5 4 3
♡ K 4
♢ A J 3
♣ 4

♠ - - -
♡ J 9 8
♢ Q 7 6 5 2
♣ K Q J 6 5

♠ 6
♡ Q 10 7 5 3
♢ K 10 9 8
♣ 9 8 3

♠ K J 9 8 2
♡ A 6 2
♢ 4
♣ A 10 7 2

West	North	East	South
		No	1♠
No	2NT (1)	No	4♠ (2)
No	5♢ (3)	No	5♡ (3)
No	6♠	All pass	

(1) Jacoby 2NT
(2) Weak
(3) Cue-bid

We have a difference of opinion whether a 6♣ cue should be bid rather than 5♡. Your excellent book on page 21 says, 'With two or more equal controls to show, bid cheapest first, i.e., up-the-line. If you by-pass a non-trump suit in cue-bidding, you deny the relevant control in that suit'.

Partner thinks 5♡ is the cheapest cue, while I think that bid denies first-round control in clubs. Could you please clarify?

(Name withheld)

Explanations:

Jacoby 2NT response: This is a game-forcing raise of opener's major suit. Opener is expected to rebid in a new suit to show a singleton or void, rebid 4-major with a minimum opening *and no shortage*, rebid 3♡ / 3NT with no shortage, but with extra length / extra strength, or 4♣ / 4♢ to show a second suit of K-Q-x-x-x or better.

Answer: (1) After 2NT, South should bid 3♢ to show the singleton. The 4♠ rebid shows a minimum *and* no short suit. The winning auction could then go:

North	South	*or*	North	South
	1♠			1♠
2NT	3♢		2NT	3♢
4NT	5♣ (1)		4♢ (2)	4♡ (?)
7♠	No		4NT	5♣
(1) 0 or 3 key cards			7♠	No
			(2) Cue-bid	

(2) Over 4♠, North might well bid 4NT rather than cue-bid. This area is covered in chapters 4 and 14 of *Cue-Bidding To Slams*. It is likely that 7♠ will not be reached any more as South's singleton diamond has not been disclosed.

(3) Over 5♢, the cheapest cue is 5♡ (as 5♡ is a cheaper bid than 6♣). On the other hand 6♣, a cue-bid at the six-level would promise the ♡A as well:

'A cue-bid at the five-level higher than the agreed trump suit or any cue-bid at the six-level is looking for a grand slam and consequently guarantees that no first-round controls are missing.'

Cue-Bidding To Slams, page 39

However, none of these cue-bids would give you enough information to bid 7♠ confidently.

In one of my newspaper columns, this question was posed:

The bidding goes:

West	East
1♣	1♠
4♠	4NT
5♣ (1)	5◇ (2)
5♡ (3)	?

(1) 0 or 3 key cards, clearly 3
(2) 'Do you have the ♠Q?'
(3) 'No.'

What should East do next with:

♠ A 8 6 5   ♡ K J 8   ◇ K Q J   ♣ A 10 3

The report of the deal read: 'The median score was 650 to East-West, but quite a number failed in 6♠ (and even 7♠), while 6♣ or 6NT is laydown.' After the above start our opponents bid 6♠. The West hand was:

♠ K 4 3 2   ♡ A Q   ◇ A   ♣ Q J 8 6 4 2

6♠ went one down with a spade and a club to lose. If the spades did not break 3-2, it could be even worse. With so much strength in the red suits, East should bid 6NT after finding the ♠Q missing. If West's jump to 4♠ is an 18-20 balanced hand, there is plenty of strength for 6NT. If the jump to 4♠ is based on long clubs, that will be fine for 6NT, too.

This question followed:

Hi, Ron,
Against us East bid 6NT after West had splintered with 4 ◇ over 1 ♠. Is it really so bad to splinter with a singleton ace?
Nick Fahrer of Sydney, Australia

Answer: Not at all. I like to splinter with (a) a minimum hand and a singleton ace because if partner is also minimum with high cards in the singleton suit, slam figures to be a poor bet (if partner has extras, then slam should be all right) or with (b) a singleton ace and a very powerful hand where I intend to bid on anyway, even if partner signs off. The auction reported is the one our opponents produced against us.

(continuing): Would you also bid 1 ♣ : 1 ♠, 4 ♠ on, say,

♠ K J 10 5　♡ 8 3　◇ A　♣ A K Q 8 7 4

when slam may be possible opposite, say,

♠ Q 9 8 4　♡ A 7 5　◇ 8 7 5 2　♣ 5 3

Answer: But hopeless on a heart lead, which the 4 ◇ splinter is virtually certain to elicit.

Dear Ron,
I intend to use the 'new to me' 1NT opening with a 5-card major. Can you let me know the follow-up bidding, please? We play 1NT as 15-18. Suppose partner opens 1NT and I have 10 points with a 4-4-4-1 pattern. Do I endeavour to play in a major? What if my hand pattern is 4-3-3-3 with four clubs? Should I look for a 5-3 major fit?

(Name withheld)

Answer: With a 4-4-4-1, 4-4-3-2 or 5-3-3-2 pattern, it is sensible to look for a 5-4, 4-4 or 5-3 major fit. With a 4-3-3-3 pattern, you might wish to find a 4-4 major fit if possible, but if your 4-card suit is a minor, you should stick with no-trumps. A 5-3-3-2 pattern facing a 4-3-3-3 will usually produce the same number of tricks in no-trumps as in a trump contract. If that number is nine, you want to be in 3NT.

Once you have decided to include a 5-3-3-2 pattern with a 5-card major in your 1NT opening, you will want a method to locate the 5-card major with opener. These are some options:

(1) Use simple Stayman. Opener treats a 5-card major as a 4-card major when replying to 1NT : 2♣. In this case you will not know whether a 5-card major is held or not. Quite a few top pairs use this and live with this defect.

(2) Play some version of 5-card major Stayman. A basic approach could start like this:

1NT : 2♣
?

    2♡ = 5 hearts
    2♠ = 5 spades
    2♢ = no 5-card major

1NT : 2♣
2♢ : ?

    2♡ = 4 hearts, inviting game
    2♠ = 4 spades, inviting game
    2NT = no 4-card major, inviting 3NT
    3♣ = forcing to game, asking for a 4-card major

Using this method, 1NT : 2♣ asks for a 5-card major and 1NT : 2♣, followed by 3♣ asks for a 4-card major. This is pretty easy to remember. Further benefits are possible. Over 3♣, opener can bid 3♡ or 3♠ to show a 4-card major and a doubleton outside, while 3♢ shows a 4-3-3-3 pattern. This will enable the partnership to play in a 4-4 fit when that is attractive and to play in 3NT when you have a 4-3-3-3 facing a 4-3-3-3.

Chapter 9: Questions on competitive bidding

1. Pairs, Dealer East : N-S vul.	What should West do with:

West   North   East   South
                1♣   1♠
?
    (See page 88)
	♠ - - -
	♡ K 10 9 6
	♢ A Q 9 5 4 3 2
	♣ K 9

2. Teams, Dealer West : E-W vul.	What should North do with:
West North East South 1♡ 2♢ 3♡ 3♠ 4♡ ? (See pages 89-92)	♠ Q 6 5 ♡ Q J ♢ A J 9 8 4 ♣ K 7 6

3. Pairs, Dealer North : Love all	East's next move with:

West   North   East   South
      1♠   Dble 2♠
No   No   ?
   (See pages 93-94)
	♠ - - -
	♡ A Q J 5 3
	♢ A J 8 6
	♣ A Q J 5

4. Pairs, Dealer South : Love all	What should West do with:

West   North   East   South
                   2♠ (1)
?
(1) Weak two opening
    (See page 97)
	♠ 9
	♡ 7 4
	♢ A K Q J 10
	♣ A J 5 4 3

5. Pairs, Dealer West : Love all	What should North do with:
West North East South 2♢ (1) ? (1)Multi-2♢, possibly weak 2♡ or 2♠ (See pages 99-100)	♠ 8 ♡ A 10 7 6 5 3 2 ♢ K Q 2 ♣ 7 3

Hello,

I'd like to solicit your opinion on these hands:

East dealer : North-South vulnerable

West	East
♠ ---	♠ J 8 6 5
♡ K 10 9 6	♡ A Q
◊ A Q 9 5 4 3 2	◊ J 10 7
♣ K 9	♣ A J 10 3

West	North	East	South
		1♣	1♠
Dble	2♠	No	No
?			

West's double was negative, looking for a possible 4-4 heart fit and leaving other options open. Do you agree with West's initial double? How do you think the bidding should proceed? Out of eight times this deal was played in my section one pair bid and made the slam. 3NT +430 and 5◊ +440 were the common scores.

Mark Niemi of Cleveland, USA

Answer: West is much too strong for a negative double when holding a long suit as well. West should start with 2◊. The bidding might then proceed:

West	North	East	South
		1♣	1♠
2◊	2♠	No	No
3♡	3♠	4◊	No
4♠ (1)	No	5♣ (2)	No
6◊	No	No	No

(1) Cue-bid, first-round control in spades
(2) Cue-bid, first-round control in clubs

The bidding would be the same if North passed 3♡.

Hi, Ron,

Playing IMPs, white against red, you are dealt as South:

♠ A K 8 7 4 2
♡ 8
♢ 6 2
♣ A 8 4 3

The auction proceeds:

West	North	East	South
1♡	2♢	3♡	?

You and partner have played several times before, but this is not a long-term partnership. You and partner are advanced and each believes the other is reasonably competent. What is the correct bid? What should it mean to partner?

Sam Graham of Germantown, Tennessee, USA

Answer: Bid 3♠. Change of suit should be played as forcing here. Partner should assume you have a good hand with 6+ spades or five very good spades. Double should be played for takeout here, but this is not appropriate with such long spades. Is 3♡ a limit raise or pre-emptive? If they are bidding significantly beyond their high card means, they will have good shape as compensation. On a bad day, you may not be able to defeat even 4♡.

(continuing): The auction proceeds:

West	North	East	South
1♡	2♢	3♡	3♠
4♡	?		

What should North do with:

♠ Q 6 5
♡ Q J
♢ A J 9 8 4
♣ K 7 6

Answer: They have bid game on light values and therefore great shape (see previous answer). 4♠ is the obvious bid. You must not pass in a competitive auction when you have undisclosed support for partner.

(continuing): In your approach to bridge, how likely/possible is it that the 3♠ bid could be made with:

♠ A J 10 7 3 2   ♡ 8 5   ◇ 6   ♣ 10 5 3 2

Answer: Certainly possible at this vulnerability (and even more reason for the other hand to bid 4♠).

(continuing): The auction proceeds:

West	North	East	South
1♡	2◇	3♡	3♠
4♡	No	No	?

What should you do now with:

♠ A K 8 7 4 2
♡ 8
◇ 6 2
♣ A 8 4 3

Answer: Double to show values. On their bidding you cannot be loaded with trumps and so you are just showing a strong hand and expecting 4♡ to fail.

(continuing): I passed out 4♡ and this was the actual deal (see opposite). *Who failed where?*

Answer: North for not bidding 4♠ (automatic). South for not doubling 4♡ (over which North should then bid 4♠).

Dealer West : East-West vulnerable

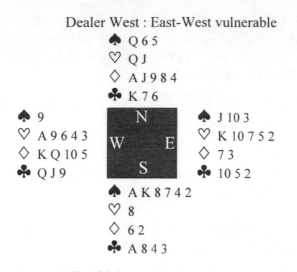

        ♠ Q 6 5
        ♡ Q J
        ♢ A J 9 8 4
        ♣ K 7 6

♠ 9   ♠ J 10 3
♡ A 9 6 4 3   ♡ K 10 7 5 2
♢ K Q 10 5   ♢ 7 3
♣ Q J 9   ♣ 10 5 2

        ♠ A K 8 7 4 2
        ♡ 8
        ♢ 6 2
        ♣ A 8 4 3

(continuing): Should the auction have been stopped somewhere to ask about the opponent's bidding? If so, when? By whom?

Answer: If either North or South needed to know, they should have asked when it was their turn to bid. Over 2♢, most would play 3♢ as a limit raise, or stronger, of opener's suit and 3♡ as a weak, pre-emptive bid.

(continuing): Does the Law of Total Tricks apply here?

Answer: Yes, in the sense that East-West have ten trumps and so should contract for ten tricks. There are 19 total trumps and so it is no surprise that one side makes ten tricks and the other side makes nine. No matter which side can make ten tricks, it is right to bid 4♠. You might meet some who do not use 3♡ as pre-emptive, but here is another possible layout where the jump to 3♡ is a limit raise (see next page). Again 4♠ is where you want to be.

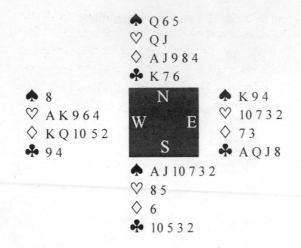

```
                    ♠ Q 6 5
                    ♡ Q J
                    ◇ A J 9 8 4
                    ♣ K 7 6
    ♠ 8                 N              ♠ K 9 4
    ♡ A K 9 6 4                        ♡ 10 7 3 2
    ◇ K Q 10 5 2    W       E          ◇ 7 3
    ♣ 9 4               S              ♣ A Q J 8
                    ♠ A J 10 7 3 2
                    ♡ 8 5
                    ◇ 6
                    ♣ 10 5 3 2
```

Dear Ron,
  Consider the following competitive sequences:

(a)   West   North   East   South
         1♣   1♠   Dble   2♠

(b)   West   North   East   South
         1♣   1♠   Dble   No
         1NT   No   2♣   2♠

(c)   West   North   East   South
         1♠   Dble   2♠

(d)   West   North   East   South
         1♠   Dble   No   2♡
         No   No   2♠

  Does the delayed raise in (b) and (d) show a weaker or a stronger hand? How do the raises differ?

                                        (Name withheld)

92

Answer: The immediate raise is stronger and suggests that responder will not be dismayed if opener continues to 3♠ in a competitive auction. The delayed support strongly suggests that responder does not wish to venture beyond the two-level, Either responder is 4-3-3-3 or has defensive prospects at the three-level. In auction (b) it is possible that responder would have been happy to defend against 2♡, but not against 2♣.

Ron,

Any chance that you give me your view on how the following hands might be bid:

West		East	
♠ K 10 4		♠ - - -	
♡ 9 7 2		♡ A Q J 5 3	
◇ 5 4 2		◇ A J 8 6	
♣ K 6 3 2		♣ A Q J 5	

West	North	East	South
	1♠	Dble	2♠
No	No	?	

What action should I take as East?

Ann Fitzgerald of Kerry, Ireland

Answer: The reasonable choices are:

● Double (again). This is the best move as it brings all suits into play and may allow you to stop in 4♣ or 4◇.

● Bid 3♠, forcing to game, reasonable with only four losers and a void in their suit. You might not make game, but the risk is reasonable. I would not mind 3♠, but it can make it harder to find a heart fit if one exists.

● Bid 3♡. This promises 5+ hearts, and that is good, but it also suggests a one-suiter (not so good, since the right spot could be in either minor).

(continuing): What should partner do next?

Answer: The bidding might go:

West	North	East	South
	1♠	Dble	2♠
No	No	Dble	No
2NT (1)	No	3♥ (2)	No
4♥	No	No	No

(1) Spades stopped, 6-9 points likely
(2) Promises five hearts

If West chose 3♣ (or 3◇) rather than 2NT, East should still bid 3♥ to try for a heart fit before committing the partnership to a minor suit. West should definitely raise to 4♥, as 3♣ or 3◇ has promised no values at all and West has support plus two kings.

Outcome: This deal caused so much debate. Contracts included 3♣, 4♣, 4♥, 4♠ (doubled and down after a 4♥ bid) and 5♣ with an overtrick.

Hi, Ron,

I was teaching a group of novices and one of them asked me what a cue-bid meant in an auction such as:

West	North	East	South
1♥	No	No	2♥ ...

I'd play 2♥ as Michaels in second seat, but as I understand it, conventional wisdom says that everything changes in the protective seat. There 2NT is natural, not unusual, Michaels falls away and jumps should be intermediate rather than weak.

Neil Hayward of Capetown, South Africa

Answer: It is reasonable to play this still as Michaels, but with opening bid strength. If Michaels is not in the repertoire, then perhaps the cue-bid can show a game-going hand.

Hi, Ron,

North opens 1NT (Precision System, 13-15 points). What should East do with:

♠ A
♡ A J 10 5
♢ K 9 8 6 4 2
♣ A 3

East-West play Pottage over 1NT. What would your bid be?

(Name withheld)

Answer: Playing Pottage, an overcall of 2♡ or 2♠ shows that major and a minor suit. A conservative approach would require 5+ hearts for a 2♡ overcall, but recommended is to use it even with just a good 4-card heart suit. If 2♡ is available in your style then that should be your choice. If that is not available, and 2♢ is used to show both majors, then start with a double. The hand works better with other methods such as Astro, where you can bid 2♣ showing hearts and even if partner bids 2♡, you can continue with 3♢ showing a good hand with diamonds longer than hearts.

Dear Ron,

My partner opened 1NT (15-18, may contain a 5-card major). I replied 2♣ (5-card major extended Stayman) with:

♠ 7 5
♡ J 5 3
♢ 8 5 4
♣ A Q J 6 3

Left-hand opponent came in with 2♡, natural, pass from partner, pass on my right, back to me. Does the Lebensohl system apply here, allowing me to bid 2NT and force a 3♣ bid from partner, which I will pass?

(Name withheld)

95

Answer: No, Lebensohl does not apply here.

(continuing): A natural 3♣ rebid by me sounds like a forcing bid and so seems wrong. Although I opted for 2NT, which caused no drama, in retrospect I believe Lebensohl is not on and all our subsequent bids should be natural.

Answer: 3♣ should be forcing in this situation, but not everyone would play it that way. What would a 2♣ response followed by a 3♣ rebid mean normally (without interference)? If not forcing, then 3♣ is not forcing now. If forcing, then 3♣ is forcing now, too.

2NT as a natural continuation was sensible. You could bid 3♡ if you wanted to force to game, bid 2♠ not forcing on a suitable hand or double for takeout (by agreement) with the values to invite game and no other more attractive call.

Hi, Ron,
What do you think is the best defence against a weak two?
                                            Eva of London, England

Answer: These are the methods we use:

Double = takeout

2NT = 15-18 balanced with at least one stopper in their suit. Over this use the same methods as after your 2NT opening.

Suit overcall = natural, about 6-7 losers.

Jump-overcall to 3♠ over their 2♡ = strong, about 5-6 losers.

Bid their suit = too strong for a minor suit overcall and asks for a stopper for 3NT.

Jumps to 4♣/4♢ = Leaping Michaels, showing about 5 losers with 5+ in the minor bid and 5+ in the other major.

After double and pass by the next player:

3-suit = useful values (8-11 points).

2NT forces 3♣, then 3-suit below opener's suit = weak (0-7).

3NT = stopper in their suit, no 4-card major.

3-their-suit = no stopper in their suit and no 4-card major.

2NT then 3NT = stopper in their suit and four cards in the other major.

2NT then 3-their-suit = 4-cards in the other major, but no stopper in their suit.

Hi, Ron,

My partner and I need help to establish the best system to cope with the following problems after a weak two-opening by the opposition. How should the bidding go for the following hands if South starts with a weak 2♠?

Bill Turner of Bridgend, Wales

(1) West   East
    ♠ 9   ♠ K 7 6 5
    ♡ 7 4   ♡ A K 5 2
    ♢ A K Q J 10   ♢ 7 5 2
    ♣ A J 5 4 3   ♣ 10 7

Answer: Our approach after a weak two is 2NT 15-18 (then 3♣ is 5-card major Stayman), double is for takeout, jumps to 4♣/4♢ are 'Michaels' (5+ in the minor bid and 5+ in the other major), while bidding their suit at the three-level is a stopper ask, usually with a hand too powerful for a 3♣ or 3♢ overcall.

On the above layout, West should bid 3♢ over 2♠ and East should bid 3NT. That is as good a spot as any, though it might fail on a non-spade lead.

(2)   West   East
       ♠ 2   ♠ 8 4
       ♡ K 5   ♡ Q 8 6 4
       ◇ A K Q J 4   ◇ 7 6 5 2
       ♣ A Q 8 6 5   ♣ J 7 3

Answer: This time West is too strong for 3◇ or 3♣. One might take a chance and bid 3♠, hoping to hear 3NT. More precise would be to double first. If you play a variation of 2NT Lebensohl here in reply to the double, that is what East would do, intending to remove the 'forced' 3♣ to 3♡ to show a poor hand with 4+ hearts. However, West should bid 3◇ over 2NT, thus indicating a hand too strong to take the 3♣ puppet. East should pass 3◇.

For West to double 2♠ and rebid 3♠ if East bids 2NT, West should have almost game-forcing values. This West is close to 3♠, but not close enough. The 3◇ rebid shows a strong hand and leaves it to partner to decide whether the values held justify pushing on. East does not have such values.

(3)   West   East
       ♠ 8 6   ♠ Q 10
       ♡ A J 7 5 3   ♡ Q 10 4
       ◇ A K 10 6 5   ◇ Q J
       ♣ 3   ♣ A Q J 6 4 2

We found the best contract of 4 ♡ after:

West	North	East	South
			2♠
No	No	3♣	No
3♡	No	4♡	All pass

but I was not happy with our bidding sequence.

Answer: Our bidding would go (2♠) : 4♢ (Leaping Michaels) showing 5+ diamonds and 5+ hearts. This is risky, but that's life. East would bid 4♡. None of us would want to pass 2♠ with those West cards and one should sooner double or bid 3♡ than pass.

(continuing): I accept that a weak 2♠ opening does a good pre-emptive job, but feel that there has to be a better method against this system with these hands than just blasting into five of a minor on (1) and (2), when these contracts fail.

Answer: With length in one or both minors the first priority is to try for 3NT. That is why East bids 3NT on (1). With an even shapelier minor suit hand, say, 6-5 or 6-6, you can bid 4NT to show both minors, but neither of the first two hands is strong enough to justify that.

Hi, Ron,
You are in second seat, nil vulnerable. The dealer opens 2♢, a multi with a weak two in either major as one of the options. What would you do with these cards:
♠ 8
♡ A 10 7 6 5 3 2
♢ K Q 2
♣ 7 3

I. McK., Australia

Answer: 2♡.

Follow-up: My concern with 2♡ was whether the hand qualifies on points or suit texture. What sort of guide do you use against multi-twos when their suit is unknown?

Answer: The basis is playing strength primarily, then hand pattern, suit length and quality, and finally points. Clearly one would pass 2♢ with:

♠ 8 5 3 2
♡ A 10 7 6
♢ K Q 2
♣ 7 3

or with:

♠ 8 3 2
♡ A 10 7 6 5
♢ K Q 2
♣ 7 3

and maybe even with:

♠ 8 3
♡ A 10 7 6 5 2
♢ K Q 2
♣ 7 3

but with:

♠ 8
♡ A 10 7 6 5 3 2
♢ K Q 2
♣ 7 3

you have only six losers and a great suit. My own test for coming in at the three-level over a weak two or a pre-empt is six losers for a takeout double or a suit overcall. A sensible guide for action at the two-level is a decent suit and seven losers and at the three-level with a decent suit and six losers. The hand you quoted is still a bit short for me to make a strong jump to 3♡. Hope trumps did not break 6-0.

Hi, Ron,

In your book, 'Bridge Conventions, Defences and Countermeasures' you present Lebensohl as a counter to their interference over a 1NT opening. Do you consider Rubensohl superior to Lebensohl?

Arch Jelley, Mt. Albert Club, New Zealand

Answer: Yes, even though Rubensohl is not widely popular. The book you mention also contains 'Transfer Lebensohl', which has a similar idea to Rubensohl.

(In Rubensohl, after 1NT and a suit overcall, responder's 2NT / 3♣ / 3♢ / 3♡ are transfers to the next suit, with the exception that the suit below the overcalled suit operates as Stayman, and opener can bid the enemy suit with no 4-card major and no stopper in their suit. In addition, responder's 3♠ = no stopper in their suit and no 4-card major, while 3NT shows a stopper in their suit, but no 4-card major. The benefits of transfers by using this approach are considerable.)

Hello, Ron,

Suppose the bidding starts:

West	North	East	South
1NT	No	No	2♡
No	No	Dble . . .	

Although you advocate double for takeout in 'Guide To Better Duplicate Bridge', we prefer penalty doubles by responder if second player intervenes. When it is the fourth player who overcalls our 1NT, should double here be for penalties or should it be treated as a re-opening double, in other words, for takeout?

BM of Heidelberg, Germany

Answer: Given that responder is relatively weak (not strong enough to invite game), it is unlikely that responder will have the trump strength suitable for a penalty double. Responder will not have five trumps (would have transferred) and so four good trumps is the best possible holding. With such trumps sitting under declarer, this is not very appealing when the points are roughly equal between the two sides.

Of course, you may choose whichever methods you wish, but I would be opting for double by responder in this position to be competitive, with two cards in the opponent's suit (perhaps even just one trump), while a suit bid would be natural (a 4-card major at the two-level since you did not transfer) and 2NT to be for the minors.

Opener is allowed to pass the double with a strong 4-card holding sitting over the bidder. How much better to be defending when the trump suit is in (a) than it is in (b) here:

(a)	Dummy		(b)	Dummy	
	x x			x x	
K J x x		x x	x x		K J x x
	A Q 10 9 x			A Q 10 9 x	

In addition we do not bar opener from taking action (such as a takeout double if holding a doubleton in their suit) in the sequence you give or similar ones.

Hi, Ron,
  You said that after I open 1NT and an opponent overcalls, my double is best used as takeout, but what if it is my partner who doubles, such as 1NT : (2 ♡) : double? Or if they open, I overcall 1NT, third hand bids something and partner doubles?
                    George Biro of Sydney, Australia

Using a takeout double by responder after opener has started with 1NT has more frequent applications, but the choice is naturally up to your partnership. This applies whether the 1NT by your side is an opening bid or an overcall. It is sensible to treat a 1NT overcall by your side as though you had opened a strong 1NT and use the same bidding structure after that as you use after a 1NT opening.

6. Teams, Dealer East : Game all	What should North do with:
West North East South 3♣ 3♡ No ? *(See page 104)*	♠ A 6 3 2 ♡ 9 8 6 4 ◇ K 5 3 ♣ 9 4

7. Pairs, Dealer South : Game all	What should South do with:
West North East South No 3♣ Dble No ? *(See pages 105-107)*	♠ A 10 5 ♡ A J ◇ J 7 6 ♣ 7 6 4 3 2

8. Teams, Dealer West : N-S vul.	What should East do with:
West North East South No No 1♣ (1) 2◇ (2) Dble (3) 5◇ ? (1) Big club (2) Weak jump (3) Takeout *(See pages 108-109)*	♠ Q 9 3 ♡ K Q 8 6 5 ◇ - - - ♣ A K Q 9 4

9. Teams, Dealer East : E-W vul.	What should South do with:
West North East South 1♡ No No Dble 2♡ ? *(See pages 111-112)*	♠ 10 9 8 ♡ A Q 7 6 ◇ A 9 3 ♣ 10 9 3

Hi, Ron,

The following deal at Imps was a problem for my partner and me:

Dealer East : Game all

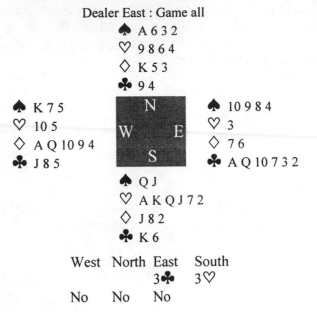

♠ A 6 3 2
♡ 9 8 6 4
◇ K 5 3
♣ 9 4

♠ K 7 5   ♠ 10 9 8 4
♡ 10 5   ♡ 3
◇ A Q 10 9 4   ◇ 7 6
♣ J 8 5   ♣ A Q 10 7 3 2

♠ Q J
♡ A K Q J 7 2
◇ J 8 2
♣ K 6

West	North	East	South
		3♣	3♡
No	No	No	

This was a bad result for us as 23 pairs reached game. Only two of those received a 3♣ opening by East. With 9 losers and only two cover cards partner did not have enough to raise to 4♡. Had she known I had six hearts, she would have deducted a loser for the super-fit and bid 4♡ confidently.

Had East passed we would have bid 1♡ : 3♣ (Bergen, 6-9 points and 4+ support), 4♡. In view of the pre-empt, how could we have reached 4♡ other than by my bidding 4♡ at once, which does not seem right in second seat. I might have considered 4♡ in fourth seat.

Arthur Schein of Sacramento, USA

Answer: 3♡ is certainly enough on your cards. Partner might have raised to 4♡ as the cards are primary (ace and king) and the 4-card support is very attractive. A three-level suit bid over a pre-empt is commonly a 6-card suit, more often than just five.

Without the pre-empt the game is not so great. Even if the spade finesse works, you still need both the diamond finesse and the club finesse. After the pre-empt every finesse is likely to work. The 3♣ opening certainly did make it awkward. The opener has only a 6-card broken suit and has four spades as well. Little wonder that so few opened 3♣.

Hi, Ron,
Pairs, both sides vulnerable. You are South with:
♠ A 10 5
♡ A J
♢ J 7 6
♣ 7 6 4 3 2
The bidding goes:

West	North	East	South
			No
3♣	Dble	No	?

Do you bid or pass?

Mark Niemi of Cleveland, USA

Answer: I bid 3♠ before reading on.

Continuing: With my club holding I envisioned West taking at least seven tricks (a maximum of +500 for us) and perhaps even more if partner is not so strong. I bid 3♠, thinking it was likely we had a 600+ game. Partner raised to 4♠. This was the full deal:

Dealer South : Game all

♠ K Q 7
♥ K Q 10 6 5
♦ A K Q 4
♣ 9

♠ 6 3
♥ 8 7 2
♦ 9 3
♣ A K Q J 8 5

♠ J 9 8 4 2
♥ 9 4 3
♦ 10 8 5 2
♣ 10

♠ A 10 5
♥ A J
♦ J 7 6
♣ 7 6 4 3 2

Do you agree with North's double? Is there a better action?

Answer: Agree with double. If you had better clubs and could leave it in, you would score more than the game is worth. North should bid 4♥ over 3♠. North is too strong for an immediate 4♥. Double followed by 4♥ shows the extra strength. To bid 4♣ over 3♠ would, with us, be a slam invitation in spades. That would be justified if North had a fourth spade.

(continuing): And can N-S sensibly reach the excellent heart slam, which depends basically on a 4-2 or 3-3 trump break?

Answer: It is too tough to find 6♥ after the 3♣ opening. Firstly, finding a slam on a 7-card fit is always tough. Secondly, after a pre-empt your first priority is to reach the best game. Thirdly, the slam is good only because you have the ♦J. Remove that card and 6♥ is anti-percentage.

Still, your best hope for finding 6♡ is for North to double and rebid 4♡ over 3♠. If 4♡ does not appeal, South might still be able to remove it to 4♠ or 5◇.

Post script: The lack of any trump winner makes one reluctant to leave the double in, but on further reflection it is best for South to pass for penalties. There is some risk attached, but on the Law of Total Tricks it is virtually certain that neither side has a 9-card trump fit. On that basis, 3♣ is highly likely to fail and there is no guarantee that N-S have game anywhere. Because North is so strong, 3♣ doubled goes for 800, but the same could ensue if North is weaker. If you swap North's ♡K for East's ♠2, no one would quarrel with double by North. Now you still score 800 from 3♣ doubled, with no game attractive for North-South, although game can be made.

Hi, Ron,

Need a takeout double of 4♡ always show spades? Would you use 4NT for the minors and forego the chance to defend 4♡ doubled, left in by partner?

George Biro of Sydney, Australia

Answer: The expectation when doubling 4♡ for takeout is that the doubler has four spades. If you double for takeout when short in spades (two or fewer), you must be prepared to have a safe place to which to run if partner does bid 4♠.

West	North	East	South	Most would play 4NT here as RKCB for spades, not a takeout for the minors.
4♡	Dble	No	4♠	
No	4NT . . .			

West	North	East	South	You can play 5♣ or 5◇ as natural, denying spade support, but make sure both partners do not take it as a cue-bid with spade support.
4♡	Dble	No	4♠	
No	5♣/5◇ . . .			

Hi, Ron,

Playing teams, they are vulnerable, you are not. The bidding starts:

West	North	East	South
No	No	1♣ (1)	2♦ (2)
Dble (3)	5♦	?	

(1) Strong club system
(2) Weak jump
(3) For takeout

What would you do as East with:

♠ Q 9 3
♡ K Q 8 6 5
♦ - - -
♣ A K Q 9 4

(Name withheld)

Answer: If double in your methods would be for takeout, that would be best. You want partner to bid if holding nothing in diamonds and to pass with some (wasted) values in diamonds. Using double for takeout whenever the opponents pre-empt or when they give an immediate raise of partner's suit is a sensible agreement.

Most would play double here for penalties and you should not do that without any values in diamonds. Given the strength revealed by your side, pass should be forcing here, leaving it to partner to bid or double. However, given the opponents are bidding to the five-level at unfavourable vulnerability with less than half the HCP, you can be sure that they have very shapely hands. On that basis it can easily be best to bid 5♡, hoping that this will work out (it should be a reasonable spot if partner has a normal takeout shape) or if not, that it might be a cheap save if it happens that they can make 5♦.

*(continuing): I doubled 5 ◇, which made when we had 5 ♡
on, which was bid at the other table. This was the full deal:*

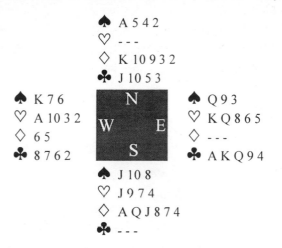

```
              ♠ A 5 4 2
              ♡ - - -
              ◇ K 10 9 3 2
              ♣ J 10 5 3
 ♠ K 7 6          N          ♠ Q 9 3
 ♡ A 10 3 2    W     E       ♡ K Q 8 6 5
 ◇ 6 5                       ◇ - - -
 ♣ 8 7 6 2        S          ♣ A K Q 9 4
              ♠ J 10 8
              ♡ J 9 7 4
              ◇ A Q J 8 7 4
              ♣ - - -
```

Post script: The North-South hands are highly distributional,
as expected. 5♡ can be defeated, but it would still be a good
sacrifice against 5◇.

Dear Ron,

*This a query where my partner and I sort of agree, but also
disagree, on the Rule of 10 and the Rule of 12, since they
really overlap, but my partner insists that both rules must be
used together. I maintain that I can double a low-level
contract with length in the suit as per the Rule of 12 and do
not believe the double has to adhere to both rules. In other
words, I think that if a hand does not fall into the Rule of 10
category, it may still fall into Rule of 12. I have successfully
doubled a low-level contract with four smallish trumps.
Could you please clarify this point for us?*

Louise Payne of England

Explanation: For those not familiar with these rules, they deal with the requirements for a low-level penalty double of a suit contract (or a penalty pass of partner's takeout double in the same zone). There are three requirements for a successful penalty double or penalty pass at a low-level:

- You have strength and length in their trump suit, and

- Your side has more points than their side, and

- You have a misfit with partner's suit(s).

What qualifies as a strong trump holding? That's where the Rules of 10 and 12 come in.

*Rule of 10: When contemplating a penalty double of a suit below game, add your expected **trump tricks** to the number of tricks the opponents are trying to win. If the answer is 10 or more, you have the right number of trump tricks. If the answer is below 10, your double is not sound.*

*Rule of 12: When contemplating a penalty double below game, add the **number of trumps** you hold to the number of tricks the opponents are trying to win. If the answer is 12 or more, you have enough trumps to play for penalties. If the answer is below 12, you do not have enough trumps.*

For example, to play for penalties at the one-level (seven tricks), you should have five trumps (Rule of 12) including three trump tricks (Rule of 10). At the two-level, four trumps and two trump tricks is the minimum recommended. Now that we are all familiar with these rules:

Answer: Yes, your trumps must satisfy *both* rules 10 and 12 to qualify as a sound penalties hand. Your good result with four low trumps was a lucky one.

110

Hello, Ron,

I would be grateful if you could give me your view on the bidding on this deal from a national championship:

Dealer East : East-West vulnerable

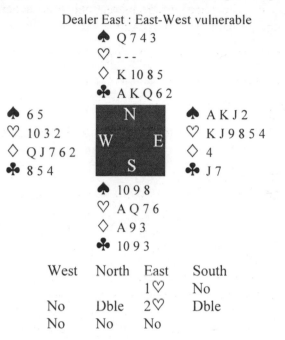

```
                    ♠ Q 7 4 3
                    ♡ - - -
                    ◇ K 10 8 5
                    ♣ A K Q 6 2
♠ 6 5                  N              ♠ A K J 2
♡ 10 3 2                              ♡ K J 9 8 5 4
◇ Q J 7 6 2      W        E           ◇ 4
♣ 8 5 4                               ♣ J 7
                       S
                    ♠ 10 9 8
                    ♡ A Q 7 6
                    ◇ A 9 3
                    ♣ 10 9 3
```

West	North	East	South
		1♡	No
No	Dble	2♡	Dble
No	No	No	

They were vulnerable, so I passed the double and it made. At the time I thought this was just a bit unlucky, but now I'm not so sure. Should South double with just the four trumps? And should North take out the double with the actual hand?

N. H., Australia

Answer: While the South trumps do qualify under the Rule of 10 and 12 (see opposite page) and although North-South figure to have more points than East-West, South should not be doubling for penalties here.

111

East-West are vulnerable and East has bid 2♡ opposite a partner known to be very weak. East knows that he is missing ♡A-Q and so South has no nasty surprise for East. If South had ♡A-Q-10-9 there might be case. Even then a penalty double would be dubious since South has terrible shape. One of the requirements for a successful low-level penalty is a misfit with partner's suit(s) (see page 110). Usually a low-level penalty requires the doubler to have exceptionally strong trumps (perhaps strong enough to draw declarer's trumps) or the ability to ruff declarer's winners. The South hand can do neither of these and so South should bid 2NT, which North can raise to 3NT (or bid 3♡ to show a strong hand, but warn partner of the heart shortage, over which South would still bid 3NT).

If you play that South's double here is for penalties, then North should be passing most of the time, but a void in trumps is a significant drawback to low-level penalties. Partner will not have more trumps because you are void. It is usually dummy who will have more trumps than expected. I would have removed the double to 3♣ because my defensive values are modest and most of my strength is concentrated in one suit. Note that North could have had ♢K-Q-J-10 and a 17-count and 2♡ doubled would still succeed.

Post script: Because a re-opening double can be very weak, a better action by North after South doubles for penalties is to bid 3♡ rather than 3♣. This shows a desire to play for game (and South will bid 3NT), but a reluctance to try for penalties.

Chapter 10: Queries on play and defence

1.

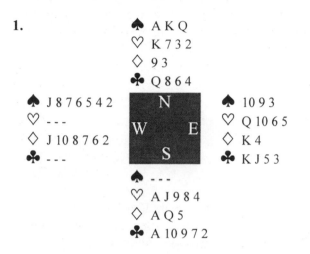

```
              ♠ A K Q
              ♡ K 7 3 2
              ◇ 9 3
              ♣ Q 8 6 4
♠ J 8 7 6 5 4 2          ♠ 10 9 3
♡ - - -                  ♡ Q 10 6 5
◇ J 10 8 7 6 2           ◇ K 4
♣ - - -                  ♣ K J 5 3
              ♠ - - -
              ♡ A J 9 8 4
              ◇ A Q 5
              ♣ A 10 9 7 2
```

South is in 6♡ on the ◇J lead: three – king – ace. Can you find a line to make 6♡ double dummy? *(See pages 117-119)*

2.

West	East
♠ K 8 5	♠ A Q 4 2
♡ K J 7 6 4	♡ 9 5 2
◇ 9 4	◇ A K J 6
♣ A K 9	♣ 10 7

West is in 4♡ on the ◇Q lead, with no opposition bidding. How would you plan the play to make the contract, with overtricks of no concern? At the table West took the lead in dummy, crossed to the ♣A and led a low heart towards the nine. What do you think of that line? *(See pages 122-124)*

Hi, Ron,

In one of your bridge columns you said, 'As usual when you cannot capture an opponent's trumps by finessing, you need to reduce your trump length.' Can you please explain why?

Dave Hurst, ex Wigan, now of Darwin, Australia

Answer: Suppose the trump layout looks like this:

```
                Dummy
                5 3
West                        East
6                           K 9 8 7
                You
                A Q J 10 4 2
```

You finesse the queen, return to dummy via another suit and finesse the jack, finding the 4-1 break. If you simply play other suits without reducing your trump length, then at some time you will be down to A-10-x or A-10-x-x with K-x on your right and have to play trumps. East's king will then make a trick.

To capture the king you need to reduce your trump length down to the same number as the player on your right. You will then be down to A-10 sitting over the K-x. If at trick 11 the lead is in dummy, you can play any card from dummy and over-ruff East. Alternatively if you have reached this position with three cards to go:

```
                Dummy
                Any three cards
West                        East
Any                         King-9 + any other card
                You
                Ace-10 + any other card
```

Simply exit with your other card and you must score the last two tricks no matter who wins trick 11. Notice that if you have not reduced your trumps sufficiently and reach this end position with the lead in your hand, you will fail.

```
                     Dummy
                     Any four cards
        West                      East
        Any                       K-9 + any two other cards
                     You
                     A-10-4 + any other card
```

If you now exit with your other card, you have to ruff the next card and are stuck in hand at trick 12. East will now score the king. You can find material on trump-reduction plays in Chapter 28 of *Guide To Better Card Play*.

Post script: This is one of the more fascinating positions for trump reduction:

```
                     Dummy
                     5 3 2
        West                      East
        Q J 8 6                   - - -
                     You
                     A K 10 9 7 4
```

You can afford to lose only one trump trick, but the bad news is revealed when you play the ace. With some luck and a bit of trump reduction, you may yet succeed, even though it appears that West has two unassailable trump tricks. You will need to ruff twice in your hand to bring your trumps down to West's length and cash your outside winners to leave a 3-card ending like this:

```
            Dummy
            Any
West                      East
Q J 8                     Any
            You
            K 10 9
```

If you are in hand, lead a low trump or if in dummy, ruff with a low trump. West can over-ruff, but you score the last two tricks and lose only one trump trick.

Declarer brought home his contract in a 2004 national teams selection tournament via trump reduction on this deal:

Dealer East : North-South vulnerable

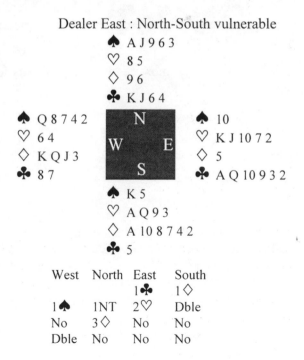

```
              ♠ A J 9 6 3
              ♡ 8 5
              ◇ 9 6
              ♣ K J 6 4
♠ Q 8 7 4 2                    ♠ 10
♡ 6 4                          ♡ K J 10 7 2
◇ K Q J 3                      ◇ 5
♣ 8 7                          ♣ A Q 10 9 3 2
              ♠ K 5
              ♡ A Q 9 3
              ◇ A 10 8 7 4 2
              ♣ 5
```

West	North	East	South
		1♣	1◇
1♠	1NT	2♡	Dble
No	3◇	No	No
Dble	No	No	No

116

West led the ♣8 and the ♣J lost to the queen. East shifted to the ◇5: two – jack – six. The ♣7 came next, ducked in dummy and ruffed by South. West's penalty double indicated the trump position, confirmed when South played the ♠K and a spade to the ace. Declarer finessed the ♡Q, cashed the ♡A and played a third heart. West discarded a spade and dummy ruffed.

A spade ruff reduced South to three trumps, leaving this ending with South on lead:

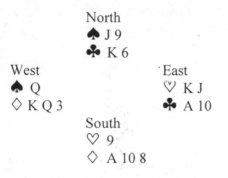

```
                    North
                    ♠ J 9
                    ♣ K 6
      West                        ·East
      ♠ Q                          ♡ K J
      ◇ K Q 3                      ♣ A 10
                    South
                    ♡ 9
                    ◇ A 10 8
```

South exited with the ♡9, West pitched the ♠Q and East won. South played a low trump on East's return to endplay West in trumps and make the doubled contract.

Dear Ron,
This deal arose in a teams event. The Deep Finesse analysis on the hand records says that a small slam makes by either North or South in clubs, hearts or no-trumps. I played it in 6 ♡ and went one off and wonder what the winning line is. Can you work it out? (See next page)

Michael Phillips of Sydney, Australia

South dealer : Love all

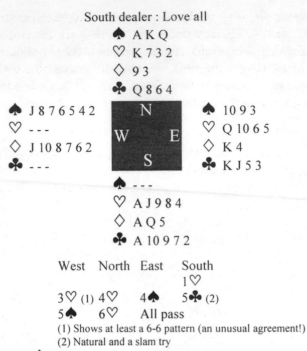

	♠ A K Q	
	♡ K 7 3 2	
	◇ 9 3	
	♣ Q 8 6 4	

♠ J 8 7 6 5 4 2   **N**   ♠ 10 9 3
♡ - - -   **W**   **E**   ♡ Q 10 6 5
◇ J 10 8 7 6 2   **S**   ◇ K 4
♣ - - -   ♣ K J 5 3

	♠ - - -	
	♡ A J 9 8 4	
	◇ A Q 5	
	♣ A 10 9 7 2	

West	North	East	South
			1♡
3♡ (1)	4♡	4♠	5♣ (2)
5♠	6♡	All pass	

(1) Shows at least a 6-6 pattern (an unusual agreement!)
(2) Natural and a slam try

Lead: ◇J: three – king – ace.

Answer: Have not looked at Deep Finesse yet, but how about
◇A, ◇Q and run the ♣10 to East to endplay East into
giving dummy an extra entry.

If East takes the club and:
(1) Exits with a club, you duck it to dummy, cash spades to
pitch two clubs and a diamond, play a low heart to the nine,
heart to the king, finesse the ♡J and cash ♡A.

(2) Exits with ♡6 or ♡5, dummy's ♡7 wins, you pitch
three clubs on the spades, finesse cheaply in hearts, ruff your
third diamond with the ♡K and finesse again in hearts.

118

(3) Exits with the ♡10 or the ♡Q, win in hand, cross to the ♡K, lead the ♣Q. If East ducks, let the ♣Q win, cash the spades, pitching two clubs and a diamond, take the heart finesse. If East covers the ♣Q, you win and the clubs are all good. Return to dummy with a club, cash a spade to discard the diamond loser and take the heart finesse.

(4) Exits with a spade, win in dummy and lead the ♣Q. Whether covered or ducked, you have access to dummy to cash the spades, pitching a diamond and two clubs if needed, followed by a low heart to the nine, back to the ♡K and repeat the heart finesse.

 If East ducks the ♣10, many lines succeed, such as heart to the king, pitch three clubs on the spades, heart finesse, ♡A, ♢Q, diamond ruff, or run the ♣9 and continue as above.

Reply: Many thanks. We looked at it for ages, including ducking the club at trick 3, but it did not seem to work. Whether one would find the winning line at the table is somewhat moot. I do not know of anyone who made the slam.

Answer: Yes, the winning lines are not obvious. It is a pretty double dummy problem. Single dummy you almost certainly will fail, as a heart to the king at trick 2 looks the natural move, even after the given bidding. After checking with *Deep Finesse*, in addition to the earlier line, it gives this line: Win ♢A, low heart to the king, lead ♣6: jack – ace, cash ♢Q, lead ♣10 to ♣Q. If East takes this, East has to give dummy a cheap entry: the ♣5 is taken by the ♣7 or the ♣3 by the ♣4, then finesse the ♡9, cross to dummy in clubs, pitch the diamond loser on a spade, heart finesse. If East ducks the ♣Q at trick 5, you ditch the other clubs on the spades, etc.

Hi, Ron,

As a bridge teacher I have two problems teaching defence:
(1) 'Standard' signals are high-encourage (discards, following to partner's honour lead). This makes sense since high = big = encouraging. However, it is a complete back-flip on leads where you lead low (or 4th highest) to say you like the suit. My students are consistently confused about sometimes low = like, and sometimes high = like. It would seem the best method is low-encourage, so that low = like always applies (whether leading, discarding or following partner's honour lead). So how then did high-encourage get the original vote being the 'Standard' signal?

S.R. of Australia

Answer: Low-encourage is definitely superior for attitude signals and also when giving count to show an even number. High-encourage is taught to beginners because it is felt that they would not notice any low card and its significance, while a high card from partner, a ten or a nine or an honour card is an attention-grabber. After they have progressed beyond novice stage, switching to low-encourage would be worthwhile.

Leading the fourth-highest card is not of itself encouraging. It has a different purpose (see later). One leads the four from 10-7-5-4-2, but that suit has little to commend it other than length. When shifting to a new suit in the middle-game, it is true that a low-card lead shows interest in the suit led, while a high-card switch denies interest in the led suit. This does not necessarily apply to the opening lead. There is another area where there is a sharp but logical distinction to the card played: we lead top-of-sequence, but in third seat follow with lowest-of-sequence when playing third-hand-high. Thus the queen is led from Q-J-10-x, but it is different in this position:

	Dummy	East would play the ten in third seat.
	8 7 4	The card played as third-hand-high
West	East	denies the next lower card, while
2 led	Q J 10 5	leading top-of-sequence denies the
		next higher card.

As one teacher has put it, lead a leader (top) but follow with a follower (lowest of touching cards for third-hand-high).

(continuing): (2) Beginners and improvers are taught to lead fourth-highest despite having no idea why. The Rule of 11 in practice is used by advanced players because improvers have enough on their plate without having to think about a complex rule, which on most hands has no benefit. So why aren't beginners and improvers just taught to lead a low card (rather than fourth-highest) since L-L-L (lead-low-like) makes much more sense to them?

Answer: What you are saying is very sensible and such a change would not be foolish. One problem is that beginners have to go and play bridge in the outside world, where leading fourth-highest is the norm. The reason for leading fourth has only a little to do with the Rule of 11. There are players who do use attitude leads (low-card lead = strength in the suit led, high-card lead denies it), but the majority prefer to use the opening low-card lead to indicate the length of the suit. Thus leading a two, if fourth-highest, shows exactly a 4-card suit and partner can deduce the number of cards declarer has in that suit. Likewise, a three lead, if the two is not visible, can be from a 4-card or 5-card suit, but not from a 6-card suit. The Rule of 11 is incidental to leading fourths and tends to be useful only when the lead is a highish spot card, such as a 5 or higher.

Hi, Ron,

East dealer : Game all

```
                    ♠ 10 7 6
                    ♡ A Q 10 8
                    ◇ Q 5
                    ♣ Q J 8 5
   ♠ K 8 5          ┌─────────┐         ♠ A Q 4 2
   ♡ K J 7 6 4      │    N    │         ♡ 9 5 2
   ◇ 9 4            │  W   E  │         ◇ A K J 6
   ♣ A K 9          │    S    │         ♣ 10 7
                    └─────────┘
                    ♠ J 9 3
                    ♡ 3
                    ◇ 10 8 7 3 2
                    ♣ 6 4 3 2
```

West	North	East	South
		1◇	No
1♡	No	1♠	No
2♣ (1)	No	3♡ (2)	No
4♡	No	No	No

(1) Fourth-suit forcing to game
(2) Promises 3-card support, but not necessarily extra strength

Lead: ◇Q

At one table declarer stayed in dummy and led the ♡2 to the jack and queen. North played another diamond, won in dummy and declarer played another heart. Now there was no way to avoid four trump losers. One down.

Our opposition declarer played a spade to hand at trick 2 and led a low heart towards dummy. No matter what North did, declarer lost only three trump tricks for a game swing. Was that the right way to handle the trump suit at teams?

(Name withheld)

Answer: To lose no more than three trump tricks, start with a low trump from dummy at trick 2. If South plays the eight or ten or queen, cover and your worries are over. When South follows with the three, play the jack.

There will be no problem if trumps break 3-2 or South has four trumps (or even five trumps). When South has a singleton, there are two relevant cases:

```
                 North
                 ♡ A Q 10 8
West                         East
♡ K J 7 6 4                  ♡ 9 5 2
                 South
                 ♡ 3
```

Low to the nine holds the losers to three. Low from dummy and playing the jack loses to the queen, but on the next round you lead low towards the nine, which holds the losers to three whether North has four trumps or South has four (as you can lead from dummy through South next time).

```
                 North
                 ♡ A Q 8 3
West                         East
♡ K J 7 6 4                  ♡ 9 5 2
                 South
                 ♡ 10
```

With this layout, low to the nine means you have four losers. Low from dummy, covering the ten with the jack, holds the losers to three. The right play (low from dummy, covering the eight or higher or inserting the jack if South plays the three) is clear. Another advantage of low from dummy is that you have only one loser on a lucky day when the trump position is like this:

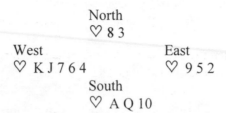

North
♡ A 8 3

West
♡ K J 7 6 4

East
♡ 9 5 2

South
♡ Q 10

Low to the nine has two losers. Low and cover the ten with the jack and you have only one loser.

North
♡ 8 3

West
♡ K J 7 6 4

East
♡ 9 5 2

South
♡ A Q 10

Low to the nine means two losers. Low from dummy, ten, jack, back to dummy and lead low again = just one loser.

Dear Ron,

When is it feasible to double to ask partner to lead dummy's first bid suit?

Ann Wardlaw of Sydney, Australia

Answer: There are two basic situations:

(1) The opponents bid to 3NT and your side has not been in the bidding. For example,

West	North	East	South
1♦	No	1♠	No
1NT	No	3NT	Dble
No	No	No	

South's double asks for a spade lead.

(2) The opponents bid freely to a slam. Double by the player not on lead asks for the lead of the first suit bid by dummy.

Hi, Ron,

(a) When leading against no-trumps with A-K-10-9-x and an outside ace as entry, should you lead top or lead the 10 from the interior sequence?

(b) When leading against no-trumps from an almost solid suit, such as A-K-J-10-x or K-Q-10-9-x, which card should you lead? You have no outside entry. If partner lacks the missing honour, should partner's card be a count card or should partner encourage / discourage?

George Biro of Sydney, Australia

Answer: (a) Normally top card is best when you have an outside ace. If you lead the 10, you might find this layout:

```
                North
                J 8 6 2
West                          East
A K 10 9 4                    5 3
                South
                Q 7
```

South wins with the queen and still has a stopper in dummy. Lead from the top and your suit sets up, with your outside ace as entry. Of course, if declarer has Q-J-x-x, leading top might not be successful. The right start can depend on the auction, what the rest of your hand looks like and whether you are playing pairs or IMPs. Top can be right also from a 4-card suit of A-K-10-9 if dummy or declarer has J-x or Q-x, while leading the 10 could give declarer an undeserved trick or a second stopper.

(b) It used to be popular to lead the ace against no-trumps to ask for an unblock and to lead the king from suits headed by A-K-J or similar. Nowadays we prefer to lead the card above the one we want partner to unblock. For example:

From A-K-Q-10-x, lead the Q, asking partner to drop the J.

From A-K-J-10-x, lead the K, asking partner to drop the Q.

From K-Q-10-9-x, lead the Q, asking partner to drop the J.

That works well since we want to lead the ace from suits headed by the A-K-J or A-K-Q. If partner has the missing honour, my lead should startle partner into remembering our agreement, since I would normally lead that honour only if I also held the card that partner has. If partner does not have the missing honour, partner should give count, preferably reverse count (high-low with an odd number, lowest from an even number).

Hi, Ron,
Can you give me your take on this deal:

Pairs : West dealer : Game all

♠ K 10 9 8
♡ A J 8
♢ Q J 6 2
♣ 4 3

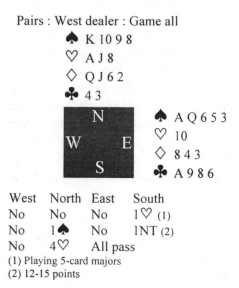

♠ A Q 6 5 3
♡ 10
♢ 8 4 3
♣ A 9 8 6

West	North	East	South
No	No	No	1♡ (1)
No	1♠	No	1NT (2)
No	4♡	All pass	

(1) Playing 5-card majors
(2) 12-15 points

126

West led the $\diamond A$ *and I played the* $\diamond 8$, *declarer the* $\diamond 7$. *I know count is best here, but we play low-encouraging on partner's lead. West switches to the* ♣7: *eight – queen – two. What do you play next?*

G.S. of Sydney, Australia

Answer: I much prefer attitude on partner's suit. Count leaves too many positions ambiguous. Reverse attitude signals, low-encouraging, high-discouraging, is superior to standard high-encouraging. Partner's ♣7, the highest spot card, will be a singleton or a doubleton and so it cannot cost to continue with the ♠A next.

(continuing): I returned a diamond. My thinking was this: There are two normal options:
(1) Play a club up to dummy's weakness. I can tell from the points revealed so far and from the bidding that partner cannot have anything in clubs, but partner does not know that I know this.
(2) Play a high spade and give partner a spade ruff.
   Why aren't I doing either of these? I could not tell whether the ♠7 *was a singleton and I did not want declarer pitching his losing diamond on the third spade when spades are 2-2. I thought he would know I had made an unusual play and if I could afford not to give him the spade ruff, I must have an outside entry, and the only possible entry can be the* ♣A. *Can we cash out or is it too hard to do? Was I expecting too much from partner? This was the complete deal.* (see over)

G.S. of Sydney, Australia

Answer: When you returned the diamond at trick 3, partner no doubt thought that you had a doubleton diamond after all and that you wanted to make sure of your two spade tricks before taking the diamond ruff.

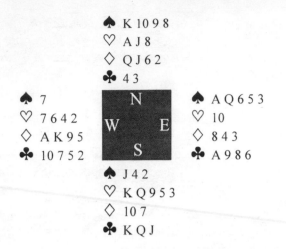

```
              ♠ K 10 9 8
              ♡ A J 8
              ◇ Q J 6 2
              ♣ 4 3
♠ 7              N           ♠ A Q 6 5 3
♡ 7 6 4 2                    ♡ 10
◇ A K 9 5   W       E        ◇ 8 4 3
♣ 10 7 5 2       S           ♣ A 9 8 6
              ♠ J 4 2
              ♡ K Q 9 5 3
              ◇ 10 7
              ♣ K Q J
```

Partner might have felt declarer's pattern was 2-5-3-3 with strong clubs, such as A-Q-J, A-K-J or even A-K-Q. In that case if you take the diamond ruff at once you can take only one spade trick. South's other spade loser would go on the fourth diamond later. On the other hand, if that is the whole scenario, partner should wonder why you did not cash the second spade before trying for the diamond ruff.

For all that, the ♠7 switch had to be from shortage and so the spades were bound to be 1-3 or 2-2 and it cannot cost to cash the ♠A first. If partner started with a singleton, you can give partner a spade ruff (with the ♠3 as a suit-preference signal for clubs) and score six tricks in all.

If spades are 2-2, South figures to be 2-5-3-3 and you will probably score only five tricks anyway. You can safely play a third spade, as declarer has no good discard. If South happens to be 2-5-2-4 and throws the diamond loser, West can ruff (it is virtually certain that partner does not have a natural trump trick) and you are still sure of coming to your ♣A.

128